Facilitation of Technology Supported Collaboration

Gert-Jan de Vreede, PhD

Robert O. Briggs, PhD

Edited by Benjamin G. Wigert

COLOPHON

Published and distributed by:

Gert-Jan de Vreede and Robert O. Briggs
The Center for Collaboration Science
University of Nebraska at Omaha
6001 Dodge Street
Omaha, NE 68182
USA

Phone: (402) 203-4481
Email: gdevreede@unomaha.edu

Cover Design by Robert H. Whitmer, Kjeldgaard Consulting, Inc.

To my wife Triparna, for her endless patience, support, and inspiration.
Gert-Jan de Vreede

To my Margaret, the love of my life, my best friend, my wife.
Robert O. Briggs

Contents

Preface

This book – *Facilitation of Technology Supported Collaboration* – is a comprehensive collection of research, field experiences, theory, expert testimonials, practical examples, and suggestions for future research from the field of collaboration science. Most importantly, it was written and organized so that the reader can develop a deep understanding of the key principles necessary for effective collaboration. As such, topics are presented in a sequential fashion with knowledge from each chapter becoming a prerequisite for fully understanding the subsequent chapter.

First, the actual social and cognitive processes behind the act of collaboration are explained. Then, a model for categorizing the fundamental layers of collaboration is presented, followed by a lengthy discussion on how facilitation enhances collaboration through the utilization of techniques considered best practices in the field. Collaboration techniques, and their theoretical underpinning, are discussed at length to provide the reader with a rich enough understanding to utilize these practices. Many examples are given to bring life the act and process of effective facilitation.

The second half of the book focuses on highlighting collaboration technology that can be used to optimize facilitated collaboration. Different technologies are described and methods for combining them with best facilitation techniques are discussed. Cases highlighting organizational use of facilitation of technology supported collaboration are also presented. The book concludes with a section on Collaboration Engineering, which is the integration of collaboration techniques and technology to best address the needs of a group and/or organization.

Facilitation of Technology Supported Collaboration is designed to provide the reader with a vast array of information necessary for understanding the foundations of effective facilitation of work groups using collaboration technologies. Furthermore, the depth, detail, and variety of practical examples included in the book make it a great resource for facilitators and collaboration designers of all skill levels. Whether you want to learn the art of facilitated collaboration, hone your skills, or seek a handbook on the best practices for collaboration, this book has something for you.

Acknowledgements

The content and materials in this book are based on past research publications and experiences. This work was conducted in collaboration with many talented colleagues and friends. We greatly appreciate their many wonderful contributions that resulted from their brilliance and enthusiastic efforts. The following authors (in alphabetical order) made major contributions to this book: Conan Albrecht, Jessica Boonstra, Alanah Davis, Douglas R. Dean, Gwendolyn Kolfschoten, Stephan Lukosch, Anne

Massey, Daniel D. Mittleman, John Murphy, Fred Niederman, Ilse Paarlberg, Doug Vogel, Jeroen Wien, Benjamin Wigert, and Wouter van Wijk.

Finally, we are deeply indebted to Benjamin Wigert who compiled and edited this book. His tireless and excellent efforts to combine, edit, and expand our various materials not only made this edition possible, but it also made it an integrated representation of years of research efforts. Any inaccuracies or errors, however, are our sole responsibility.

Gert-Jan de Vreede

Robert O. Briggs

Omaha, NE

January 2011

Chapter One

Introduction

Why is Collaboration Difficult?

In the knowledge economy, organizations frequently face problems of such complexity that no single individual has sufficient expertise, influence, or resources to solve the problem alone. Instead, organizations frequently rely on group problem solving to overcome their greatest challenges, and formulate plans for future growth (Kozlowski & Bell, 2008). Collaboration has, therefore, become a ubiquitous feature of organizational life. We define *collaboration* as joint effort toward a group goal. Groups collaborate to create value that their members cannot create through individual effort. Group decisions are expected to be of the highest quality because, ideally, group members should be able to pool their diverse knowledge and skills to come-up with better decisions than independent problem solvers. Unfortunately, this is not always the case. Collaboration engenders a set of interpersonal, social, political, cognitive, and technical challenges. Multiple actors with diverse backgrounds must establish common understandings (Weick, Sutcliffe, & Obstfeld, 2005) and align their efforts (Ren, Kiesler & Fussell 2008). They must think creatively, sometimes quickly, to solve problems (Rudolph, Morrison, and Carroll 2008) in the face of potential barriers (Ren, Kiesler, & Fussell, 2008) and distractions (Laxmisan et al., 2007).

Social Challenges

Raw group decision making efforts – unaided by either a facilitator or collaboration technology – tend to encounter major problems due to social and cognitive obstacles experienced during interpersonal interactions (see Figure 1). For example, at the team level, a social phenomenon called *production blocking* occurs when a group member cannot communicate his or her thoughts because someone else is speaking or being disagreeable (Diehl & Stroebe, 1987). Another key detriment to group decision making is evaluation apprehension, which can be problematic when members do not share suggestions with the group because they fear that they will be judged negatively by others (Diehl & Stroebe, 1987; Litchfield, 2008).

Furthermore, other social influence processes involved in group brainstorming can lead to negative occurrences in the production of high quality solutions, such as premature consensus in decision making (Aldag & Fuller 1993), focusing on common rather than unique information (Stasser & Titus, 1995), and tendencies toward agreement with consensus (Larey & Paulus, 1999). Janis (1972) warned that groupthink occurs when one succumbs to social pressure and limits ideas, solutions, and problem considerations to those commonly shared by the majority group members. Consequently, groupthink can lead to faulty conclusions because not all aspects of a problem and its potential solutions are considered.

Individual Challenges

At the individual level, one of the biggest challenges that can occur during group work is excessive cognitive load. Cognitive load becomes problematic when a group member allocates his or her attention resources to many different activities – such as listening, thinking, speaking, and retaining information from a variety of sources – to the extent that it is difficult to put everything into clear, logical thought (Paas, Renkl & Sweller, 2003).

Team Theory of Group Productivity

A popular model of team productivity called *Team Theory of Group Productivity* specifies that team member attention resources are limited, and that they are divided among three cognitive processes: communication, deliberation, and information access (*adapted from* Briggs, 1994; *as cited in* Nunamaker, Briggs, Mittleman, Vogel, & Balthazard, 1997). During communication, individuals must put cognitive effort into developing a thought, choosing words, anticipating how a message will be best received, and deciding how to deliver one's thoughts. Deliberation occurs during typical problem solving activities, such as defining the problem (e.g., considering all aspects of the problem), developing potential solutions, choosing a solution, and evaluating the effectiveness of the solution (Briggs, 1994; Dewey, 1910; Guilford, 1967; Mumford, Mobley, Uhlman, Reiter-Palmon, & Doares, 1991; Newell & Simon, 1972; Sternberg, 1986). While attention resources are being devoted to these cognitive processes, a team member must also perform information access tasks such as finding, storing, processing, and retrieving knowledge shared between team members.

Importantly, Team Theory emphasizes that information shared amongst team members is valuable to the extent that it is understood, complete, accurate, and available when it is needed (Briggs, 1994; Nunamaker et al., 1997). Thus, when social and/or cognitive obstacles impede the development of ideas at the individual level, or the sharing of ideas with team members, team decision making may be of lower quality if pertinent information possessed by a team member is not utilized. Furthermore, Team Theory suggests that the motivation to actively communicate, deliberate, and access information is influenced by goal congruence. Specifically, the theory posits that individuals with high goal congruence – "the degree to which the vested interests of individual team members are compatible with the group goal" – will be more motivated to apply effortful cognitive resources to the decision making process than those who do not share the group's objectives (Nunamaker et al., 1997, p. 166).

Figure 1: Group problem solving factors that are detrimental to solution quality (Nunamaker et al., 1997)

Overcoming Challenges with Facilitation & Technology

Given the aforementioned challenges associated with group work, it is clear that group decision making can be improved if a group can capitalize on the knowledge, skills, and abilities of its members by means of minimizing aggregate information loss due to these social and cognitive limitations. Thus, the question is, "How can the detrimental effects of these pitfalls be minimized during collaborative problem solving?" And the answer is: "Through structured *facilitation* of collaborative problem solving." Facilitation is a dynamic group decision making process conducted by a third party moderator that aims to manage interpersonal interactions, orchestrate the use of technology, and simplify group tasks through a structured decision making framework (Bostrom, Anson, & Clawson, 1993; de Vreede, Niederman, & Paarlberg, 1999). In other words, facilitation of group collaboration basically involves altering the decision making process such that 1) tasks are broken-down into smaller, simpler, independent activities (e.g., generate ideas, clarify ideas, or evaluate ideas); and 2) interpersonal conflict is minimized through communication restrictions such as anonymity of who provided an idea and rules against debating ideas.

However, facilitated collaboration is difficult. Effectively communicating pertinent instructions, monitoring participant contributions, dealing with conflict, and facilitating the flow of information/conversation is a lot to ask out of one person. Fortunately, technology can simplify and magnify the power of the facilitator and his methods! Collaboration technology, such as Group Support Systems (GSS), helps the facilitator simultaneously display tasks and instructions that group members need to understand in order to minimize the aforementioned challenges of collaboration and maximize the benefits of teamwork. In other words, this technology allows the facilitator to control what decision making tasks group members see, how they can contribute to the group, and when they can contribute. Thus, it is easier for facilitators to breakdown the collaboration process into smaller, simpler, independent activities. Technology also can be used to greatly reduce interpersonal conflict. For instance, GSS software can be configured such that participants can anonymously contribute their ideas. This anonymity reduces participants' social fears, such as being judged, retaliated against, or condemned for disagreeing with an authority figure (e.g., supervisor, boss, professor, client).

Research shows that, under certain conditions, groups can improve key outcomes using collaboration technologies (Briggs et al., 2009). Any technology that can be used well, however, can also be used badly. IS/IT artifacts do not assure successful collaboration. The value of a collaboration technology can only be realized in the larger context of a *collaboration system,* which we define as a combination of actors, hardware, software, knowledge, and work practices to facilitate groups in achieving their goals, in an effective and efficient way.

Designers of collaboration systems must therefore consider social, psychological, cognitive, technical, and many other aspects of collaboration when creating a new collaboration system. Collaboration researchers across many disciplines have produced a substantial and growing body of exploratory, theoretical, experimental, and applied research that could inform design choices. The purpose of this book is to integrate, catalogue, and clarify what we know about facilitation of technology supported collaboration. Through establishing some foundations, organizing frameworks, and approaches to the facilitation of technology supported collaboration, we aspire to advance the field of collaboration science.

Overview of Book Chapters

Chapter Two: A Seven Layer Model of Collaboration

How can designers of a collaboration process keep track of all the components and considerations that are needed to address the challenges associated with group decision making? Briggs et al. (2009) developed a Seven Layer Model of Collaboration (SLMC) to simplify this task and improve the consistency of high quality collaborative process designs. The SLMC is comprised of seven layers critical to effective collaboration: goals, products, activities, patterns of collaboration, techniques, tools, and scripts.

In Chapter Two, the development of the SLMC is described through a comprehensive explanation of the inductive and deductive reasoning behind each layer. Specifically, the most important considerations facilitators and designers of collaborative problem solving must make in regard to each layer are highlighted, and the points of validation for each layer are also argued. Furthermore, the interface between the layers is discussed.

Chapter Three: Facilitation

Chapter Three is dedicated to explaining how facilitation can alleviate many of the challenges associated with group work, while capitalizing on the diverse expertise and problem solving abilities of multiple minds. Facilitation is defined in this chapter as dynamic process that involves managing relationships between people, tasks, and technology, as well as structuring tasks and contributing to effective accomplishment of the meeting's outcome (de Vreede, 2002).

Multiple types of facilitation exist, such as 'technical facilitation' which involves the teaching of software use, and 'group process facilitation' which refers to facilitating collaborative efforts – the focus of the chapter. Three streams of facilitation research are examined, as facilitation can influence collaboration processes, outcomes, and participant satisfaction. Additionally, the four primary roles of a facilitator are identified.

The general components comprised by thinkLets are identified and explained in the chapter. Also, the benefits of thinkLet-based collaborative process designs are emphasized in the chapter. For instance, the origin of the pattern-design language used in thinkLets is communicated and the associated benefits are depicted. Furthermore, patterns of collaboration optimal for achieving a specified goal are explained. The most promising sequential interactions between different patterns of collaboration are also discussed. Chapter Three concludes with a subsection on the comparison between manual and electronic thinkLet tools.

Chapter Four: ThinkLets

It is important for facilitators to utilize techniques that effectively and consistently implement the SLMC. In this chapter we explain why and how a collection of best practices in facilitated collaboration called 'thinkLets' comes to the rescue, providing facilitators and collaboration process designers with a toolbox for understanding, designing, and executing collaborative processes. ThinkLets employ collaborative processes that encompass the patterns of collaboration showcased in the fourth layer of the SLMC. They are a repeatable pattern language that is easy to understand and in addition to outlining the steps for conducting specific collaborative processes, they give guidance for how to set-up collaboration tools that support the decision making process.

Chapter Five: ThinkLets: Patterns of Collaboration

Designing a thinkLets based process is challenging and requires knowledge of what each thinkLet can do, as well as how to integrate a combination of thinkLets to evoke the desired group behaviors. In order to fully understand the conceptual underpinnings of thinkLets, one must develop a comprehensive understanding of the patterns of collaboration that can be elicited by thinkLets. This chapter explains the six primary patterns of collaboration in detail: generate, reduce, clarify, organize, evaluate, and build consensus.

Chapter Six: Examples of ThinkLets

This chapter provides examples of a different thinkLet for each pattern of collaboration. These examples are taken directly from a collection of actual thinkLets (Briggs & de Vreede, 2009) and reflect some of the more specific information not presented in the previous chapters. For instance, an actual thinkLet will have instructions for: *when to use, when NOT to use, what should happen, what exactly a facilitator should do* (script), and *tips for success*.

Chapter Seven: Collaboration Technology

Chapter Seven entails a taxonomy of the different types of technology that can be used to support collaboration. In this chapter, based on the work of Mittleman, Briggs, Murphy, & Davis (2009), we propose a starting place toward developing such a collaboration engineering model. The purpose of this classification scheme is to provide a lens through which people can better understand the capabilities of, and relationships between, collaboration technologies. Such a framework might then help practitioners to select from among commercial collaboration software offerings, offer groupware designers a range of design choices for new systems, and reveal new challenges to the groupware research community.

Chapter Eight: Group Support Systems

Group Support Systems (GSS) is one of the leading technologies for supporting electronic facilitated collaboration. The primary benefits of utilizing GSS along with facilitation techniques include improvements in collaboration outcome quality and originality, group interactions, decision making processes, and participant satisfaction. These benefits are described in greater detail, as well as the cause and effect relationships between them.

In this chapter the tools that can be used within GSS are summarized, and a brief history of group support software is presented – including a list of buzzwords surrounding GSS. Experiences from the field and experimental findings are shared in regards to the effectiveness of GSS in different contexts. For example, the impact of group size, culture, and organization on collaboration was examined. Chapter Eight concludes with a discussion on what we can expect from meeting environments of the future.

Chapter Nine: Organizational Use of GSS

GSS have now been commercialized and are present in an increasing number of domestic and international contexts but only lightly studied in real organizational settings. A criticism of studies has been that many of the organizations involved had a vested interest in the outcome that extended beyond that which would normally occur in a typical organization. An additional challenge has been made with respect to the generalizability of field study results across corporate and national cultures. This chapter addresses many of these issues.

In order to bring examples of organizational use of GSS to life, we present a study by de Vreede, Vogel, Kolfschoten, and Wien (2003) that compares and contrasts organizational use of GSS at International Business Machines (IBM) and Boeing Aircraft Corporation in the US with those from two European companies: Nationale-Nederlanden (NN), the largest insurance firm in the Netherlands and European Aeronautic Defense and Space company, Military division (EADS-M). In this study attention is given to aspects of efficiency, effectiveness, and user satisfaction as well as group dynamics.

Chapter Ten: Collaboration Engineering

Collaboration Engineering is critical to the synergy of best practices in facilitation techniques, collaborative technology, and organizational use of collaboration. Chapter Ten addresses how Collaboration Engineering concerns the design and deployment of collaboration processes for recurring high-value collaborative tasks. In Collaboration Engineering, a *collaboration engineer* designs a reusable and predictable collaboration process for a recurring task including technological support, and transfers the design to *practitioners* to execute for themselves without the ongoing intervention of *group process professionals*, i.e. facilitators (de Vreede, Briggs, & Massey, 2009).

Specifically, the domain of Collaboration Engineering is explored, and a list of successful Collaboration Engineering initiatives conducted at highly regarded corporations is showcased. Foundations of Collaboration Engineering, such as the pattern and pattern-based designs, are emphasized. Additionally, the design and deployment phases of collaboration are delineated in great detail.

There are three primary modeling techniques that are considered best practices in Collaboration Engineering: thinkLets documentation format, facilitation process model, and agenda design format. The theoretical basis for each technique is presented and an example of each technique is depicted graphically. Chapter Ten concludes with a discussion on future research directions for Collaboration Engineering.

Chapter Eleven: Discovering and Assessing Collaboration Engineering

Before facilitation of collaborative problem solving efforts can be implemented into an organization, you must first identify where it is needed and what specifics problems exist. Furthermore, the extent of these problems and the manner in which facilitated collaboration should be instituted must be assessed. Previous research from Dean et al. (2006) suggests five criteria for identifying projects that might be conducive to a collaboration engineering intervention. These criteria include the following:

1. Clearly defined outcomes for the collaboration engineering project from the process owner.

2. Important, yet inefficient recurring processes.

3. Tasks of an appropriate type based on the interaction intensity, information processing intensity, and the number of participants.

4. Participants in the task tend to have aligned goals.

5. Champions and adequate budgets.

In this chapter we extend that work by applying the Value Frequency Model (VFM) (Briggs, 2006) for change-of-work-practice to the derivation of an interview protocol for discovering and qualifying collaboration engineering opportunities. We first define key terms and then summarize the propositions of the VFM. We next explain how the questions of the interview protocol link to the constructs of the VFM. We then report the results of two field studies we conducted where people used the protocol to discover and evaluate collaboration engineering opportunities in their own organizations. Finally, the chapter concludes by providing suggestions for future research.

Chapter Two

A Seven Layer Model of Collaboration

Why do Facilitators need a Model of Collaboration?

Finding, assimilating, and using the concepts of collaboration science can impose high cognitive load on designers, which in turn, can lead to design defects in collaboration systems (Briggs et al., 2009). This, in turn, may result in lost productivity for system users. Designers of collaboration systems may therefore find it useful to have an organizing scheme for collaboration science that affords them a separation of concerns at design time. In response to this concern Briggs et al. (2009) derived a Seven-Layer Model of Collaboration (SLMC) to afford a multidimensional separation of concerns to collaboration system designers.

In their 2009 paper, Briggs et al. identified design considerations at the interface of each layer with the layer above it. They explained the kinds of phenomena that manifest at each layer, the theories surrounding these phenomena, and approaches to measuring them. Briggs et al. argued that many collaboration technologies focus too narrowly on a few layers of the model. Thus, next generation collaboration support systems should accommodate the mobilizing of understandings at all seven layers of the model.

Development of the SLMC

Briggs et al. (2009) used inductive logic to derive the seven key areas of design concerns for collaboration systems. They gathered supporting evidence for their inductions from more than 400 collaboration science research papers in the Information Systems domain, and from several of its referent disciplines, among them Computer Science, Psychology, Management, and Education. Briggs et al. then used deductive logic to build an argument that these areas of concern address collaboration at differing levels of abstraction, and so may be organized into a seven-layer model, affording separation of concerns at design time.

Table 1 Seven Layers of the Model of Collaboration.
Adapted from Briggs et al. (2009).

Purpose of Layer for Collaboration Engineers	Layer	Description
Why?	Goals	A *goal* is a desired state or outcome. Deals with group goals, private goals, and goal congruence – the degree to which individuals perceive that working toward group goals will be instrumental to attaining private goals. Collaboration is defined as joint effort toward a group goal. Addresses motivation, group formation, commitment, productivity, satisfaction, and other goal-related phenomena
	Products	A *product* is a tangible or intangible artifact or outcome produced by the group's labor. Deals with issues of quality, creativity, effectiveness, efficiency, and other product-related phenomena.
What?	Activities	*Activities* are sub-tasks that, when completed, yield the products that constitute attainment of the group goal. Deals with what groups must do to achieve their goals: sequences of steps that constitute decision-making and problem-solving approaches.
How? (Logical Design)	Patterns of Collaboration	*Patterns of collaboration* are observable regularities of behavior and outcome that emerge over time in teamwork. Researchers address six general patterns of collaboration: Generate Reduce, Clarify, Organize, Evaluate, and Build Commitment.
	Techniques	A *collaboration technique* is a reusable procedure for invoking useful interactions among people working toward a group goal. Deals with invoking useful outcomes predictably and repeatably across a wide range of circumstances.
How? (Physical Design)	Tools	Collaboration *tools* are artifacts or apparatus used in performing an operation for moving a group toward its goals. Deals with designing, developing, deploying, and using technologies in support of group efforts.
	Scripts	A *script* is everything team members say to each other and do with their tools to move toward the group goal. Scripts may be internal or external, tacit or explicitly captured as documentation. Deals with tacit and explicit procedural guidance for the group. Small variations in structured scripts can yield substantial variations in group dynamics. .

The Goals Layer

Key Concerns for Facilitators. Many of the key concerns for successful collaboration relate to group goals, private goals, and the relationships among them. A *goal* is defined as a desired state or outcome (Locke & Latham 1990). Much research focuses on the role of goals in group formation (Hahn, Moon, & Zhang, 2008), motivation (Vroom, 1995), continuity (Lodewijkx, Rabbie, & Visser, 2006), productivity (Wheelan, 2009), and success (Levi, 2007).

Key phenomena in collaboration science are defined in terms of group goals. Collaboration itself, for example, is defined as joint effort toward a group goal (Briggs et al., 2009). Definitions of the terms, *group* and *team,* often refer to the collection of people who have committed to work toward a group goal (e.g. Cohen and Bailey 1997). The effectiveness of a group is defined in terms of the degree to which a group attains the goals toward which it works (Cohen & Bailey, 1997). Group efficiency is defined in terms of the degree to which a group conserves its resources during the attainment of a group goal (Veld, 1987).

Other collaboration concerns pertain to the private goals of individual group members. Group cohesion is sometimes measured in terms of the degree to which an individual group member desires (has a goal) to remain a member of a group (Evans & Dion 1991). The Yield Shift Theory of satisfaction (Briggs, Reinig, & de Vreede, 2008) predicts that individual team members will feel satisfied with their group to the extent that group processes and outcomes invoke shifts in the perceived utility of and likelihood of attaining private goals.

As eluded to in the introduction chapter, phenomena, such as motivation (Hayne, 1999), commitment, consensus, and willingness to change, relate to *goal congruence* – the degree to which individuals perceive that working toward group goals would be instrumental toward attaining salient private goals. Instrumentality, Expectancy, and Reasons theories of motivation posit that motivation to make effort toward group goals will be a function of the degree to which individuals perceive value or benefit in the outcomes of the behaviors the group considers enacting (Westaby, 2002). In a group setting, these perceptions pertain to the actions an individual contemplates toward helping a group attain its goals. The Instrumentality Theory of Consensus posits that individuals will only be willing to commit effort and resources toward a proposal for achieving a group goal to the extent that they perceive that outcomes of the effort would be instrumental to their salient private goals (Briggs et al., 2005). The Value Frequency Model (VFM) for Change of Work Practice posits that an individual's willingness to change to a new way of working (e.g. a new collaborative approach) will be a function of the overall positive or negative value the individual perceives in using the new work practice, and the frequency with which the individual perceives that value will be attained (Briggs et al., 2007). VFM posits six dimensions of value: Economic, political, social, cognitive, affective, and physical. These dimensions pertain directly to the kinds of utility individuals anticipate from the attainment of their salient private goals.

Issues of group formation and cohesion, efficiency and effectiveness, satisfaction, consensus, willingness to change and other goal related phenomena must be addressed by the designers of designers of collaboration systems and -related phenomena. Briggs et al. (2009) generalized these concepts into an area of concerns labeled, "Goals."

Deductive Validation of the Goals Layer. Without a group goal, collaboration does not exist (Briggs et al., 2009). Unless the private goals of the individuals are congruent with the group goal, team members will not commit to collaborate, and so the group will not exist. If a group does not exist, then there is no need to address the other areas of concern. Concerns pertaining to goals must therefore comprise the top-most layer of the SLMC, because all other layers depend on the top layer.

The Products Layer

Key Concerns for Facilitators. Designers of collaboration systems must consider a number of aspects relating to the products a group will create through its joint efforts. Much research addresses group products. A *product* is a tangible object or intangible state produced by the group's labor, the existence of which advances a group toward its goal. The goal of an internal risk audit, for example, is to discover risks that have not yet been controlled or mitigated, and to develop controls to cover those risks. The product for an internal audit could be a list of risks organized by organizational unit, evaluated for likelihood and impact, elaborated with plans to mitigate each risk, and signed off by an auditor to signify that the controls are in place and functioning properly. The existence of this constitutes the attainment of the group goal for the risk assessment. Some products that groups create directly support attainment of formal group goals. Others are useful for instrumental goals. A brainstorm on project risks, for example, could lead to an idea for process improvements that does not only control risks, but also increases efficiency.

Meta analyses covering more than 300 studies (Baltes, Dickson, Sherman, Bauer, & LaGanke, 2002; Dennis & Wixom, 2002; Fjermestad & Hiltz, 1999; Hwang, 1998; McLeod, 1992) in the collaboration literature identify a number of issues pertaining to the products of collaboration as studied in the lab and the field. Some of these issues pertain to attributes of tangible products, such as the quality of a decision (Dean et al., 2006; Kellermanns et al., 2008), and the creativity and number of solutions (Dean et al. 2006). Others pertain to intangible products like awareness of problems (Ravi Beegun & Leroy, 2009), participation (Saltz et al., 2007), or gaining multiple perspectives (Clawson et al., 1993). Still others focus on the degree to which variations in the attributes of the team (Van Knippenberg & Schippers, 2006), the task (Higgs, Plewnia, & Ploch, 2005), and in other aspects affect the attributes of group products. Briggs et al. generalized these concepts into an area of concerns labeled, "Products."

Deductive Validation of the Products Layer. To achieve their goals, groups create products – artifacts and outcomes that constitute goal attainment (Briggs et al., 2009). Until a group goal exists, one cannot assert the need for a product, nor judge the degree to which a product fulfills a goal. If a group changes its goals, it may need to change the products it will create because products are the means by which a group goal is realized. If a group creates a product that does not attain its formal or instrumental goals, that product has no purpose. Products therefore depend on goals. A group may decide to attain the same goal by creating different products. Goals are therefore independent of products. Concerns about products must therefore be subordinate to concerns about goals. Lacking a product, however, there would be no need to address concerns about activities, patterns of collaboration, techniques, tools, or scripts, because there would be no purpose to group action. The Products Layer must fall below the Goals Layer, but above the other layers in the SLMC.

The Activities Layer

Key Concerns for Facilitators. Collaboration systems designers focus much of their efforts on designing the sequence of activities through which a group moves to achieve its goals. *Activities* are sub-tasks that, when completed, yield the products that constitute attainment of the group goal. Activities reduce cognitive load by decomposing the group goal into manageable chunks, each with its own interim goals and interim products. Many researchers describe domain-specific models that decompose goal attainment into a series of generalized activities. Herbert Simon proposed an economic model for rational decision making based on the premise that people go through a series of activities when evaluating a decision (Simon, 1979). Management researchers decompose decision into variations on a set of activities typically including, problem identification, alternative generation, evaluation, and selection, planning, execution, and review (e.g. Dean & Sharfman, 1996; Mitroff et al,. 1974 Schwenk, 1984). Psychology researchers also propose activities as a foundation for problem solving tactics. For example, D'zurilla and Goldfried (1971) defined problem solving as a behavioral process which includes problem definition and formulations, generation of alternatives, evaluation and selection, and verification of potential solutions. Variations on these activities can be found throughout many literatures. The logical design phase in systems analysis and design methodologies, for example, typically include activities for problem identification, alternative generation, evaluation, and choice (Whitten, Bentley, & Dittman, 2007).

Collaboration technology researchers often discuss the capabilities of their systems in terms of the tasks or activities they support. Nunamaker, et. al. (1996) make frequent reference to the tasks and activities the users go through when using GSS software, among them idea generation, idea organization, and idea evaluation. DeSanctis and Gallupe (1987) propose that GSS should support planning, creativity, intellectual, preference, cognitive conflict, and mixed motive tasks. Using Speech-Act Theory, Flores and Winograd model collaboration processes as sequences of speech-act combinations to form standardized team activity workflows (Flores et al., 1988; Winograd and Flores 1986). Based on their modeling approach, various collaboration systems in the area of workflow management were proposed. From these related research streams Briggs et al. derived the area of concern they labeled "Activities".

Deductive Validation of the Activities Layer. Activities are sub-tasks for creating a group's products (Briggs et al., 2009). Until there is a product to create, activities have no purpose. If a group changes the product it intends to create, it will have to change its activities, because activities produce sub-products leading to the products that attain the group goal. If the product changes, the sub-products must also change, so activities depend on products. A group may decide to use different activities to create the same product however, so products are independent of activities. Concerns about activities must therefore be subordinate to concerns about products. Lacking activities, however there would be no venue for realizing patterns of collaboration, techniques, tools, or scripts. The Activities Layer must therefore fall below the Products Layers, but above the Patterns of Collaboration, Techniques, Tools, and Scripts layers of the SLMC

The Patterns of Collaboration Layer

Key Concerns for Facilitators. Collaboration researchers have addressed a number of issues pertaining to how groups move through their activities. *Patterns of collaboration* are observable regularities of behavior and outcome that emerge over time in teamwork (de Vreede et al., 2006). Collaboration engineering researchers identify identified six patterns of collaboration that characterize how groups move toward their goals (de Vreede et al., 2009).

- **Generate:** To move from having fewer concepts to having more concepts in the set of ideas shared by the group.

- **Reduce:** To move from having many concepts to a focus on fewer ideas deemed worthy of further attention.

- **Clarify:** To move from less to more shared understanding of the concepts in the set of ideas shared by the group.

- **Organize:** To move from less to more understanding of the relationships among concepts in the set of ideas shared by the group.

- **Evaluate:** To move from less to more understanding of the instrumentality of the concepts in the idea set shared by the group toward attaining group and private goals.

- **Build Commitment:** To move from fewer to more group members who are willing to commit to a proposal for moving the group toward attaining its goal(s).

Most of the behaviors in which a group engages as it moves through an activity can be characterized by these six patterns. In a risk assessment, for example, as a group moves through a risk identification activity, they may *generate* candidate risk statements, *evaluate* the likelihood and impact of each risk, and *reduce* the list to the risks that pose a credible threat to the organization.

Researchers study phenomena relating to each of the six patterns of collaboration. With respect to the *Generate* pattern, for example, studies report the number of ideas a group produces (Connolly et al. 1990), their originality, relevance, quality, effectiveness, feasibility, and thoroughness (Dean et al., 2006). People generate by creating new ideas (Reiter-Palmon et al., 1997), by gathering previously unshared ideas (Bock et al., 2005), or by elaborating on existing ideas with additional details (de Vreede et al., 1999). For the *Reduce* pattern, researchers address, for example, the number of ideas in the shared set, the degree to which a reduced idea set includes high-quality ideas and excludes low-quality ideas (Barzilay et al., 1999), and the degree to which reduction of idea sets yields reductions of actual and perceived cognitive load (Simpson & Prusak, 1995). Groups reduce idea sets through idea filtering (Chambless et al., 2005), generalizing ideas (Yeung et al., 1999) or selection (Rietzschel, Nijstad, & Stroebe, 2006).

Researchers of the *Clarify* pattern focus on, among other things, reductions in ambiguity, reductions in the number of words required to convey meaning, and establishing mutual assumptions (Mulder, et al., 2002). Among the phenomena of interest for research on the *Organize* pattern of collaboration are shared understandings of the relationships among concepts (Cannon-Bowers & Converse, 2001), cognitive load (Grisé & Gallupe 1999), and the simplicity or complexity of the relationships among concepts (e.g.

complex structures may signify sequence, hierarchy, and networks of relationships, which in turn may model, for example, semantics of chronology, composition, heredity, or causation (Dean et al., 2000)). Research on the *Evaluate* pattern addresses projections of possible consequences of choices, and the degree to which those consequences would promote or inhibit goal attainment (Westaby, 2002). Rating, ranking, and inclusion/exclusion are common means of evaluation (Gavish & Gerdes, 1997). Research on such techniques focuses, for example, on the degree to which participants can accurately project the likely outcomes of the proposals they consider (Laukkanen, Annika Kangas, & Jyrki-Kangas, 2002). Phenomena of interest for the *Build Commitment* pattern pertain to the degree to which people are willing to contribute to the group's efforts (Montoya-Weiss, Massey, & Song, 2001). Issues of commitment arise in many phases of group work, starting with the formation of the group (Datta, 2007), and continuing through every proposed course of action and every choice group members make as they move through their activities (Saaty & Shang, 2007).

Based on these streams of research, Briggs et al. induced an area of concern for designers of collaboration systems that they labeled "Patterns of Collaboration".

Deductive Validation of the Patterns of Collaboration Layer. Patterns of collaboration characterize how a group moves through its activities. Until sub-tasks have been identified and their sub-products articulated, it would not be possible to determine what combination of patterns might be useful for create a sub-product. If a group changes the sub-products it intends to create, then it may need to change the patterns of collaboration it needs to create them, because the patterns must give rise to the sub-products. Concerns about Patterns of Collaboration must therefore be subordinate to concerns about activities. Patterns of Collaboration therefore depend on Activities. A group might decide to use a different combination of patterns of collaboration to create the same sub-products. Activities are therefore independent of patterns of collaboration. Lacking patterns of collaboration, it would not be possible to select among techniques because techniques are meant to invoke patterns of collaboration. Likewise, it would not be possible to select tools or create scripts. The Patterns of Collaboration Layer must therefore fall below the Activities layers, but above the Techniques, Tools, and Scripts layers of the SLMC.

The Techniques Layer

Key Concerns for Facilitators. Researchers report many reusable collaboration techniques that groups can employ to improve group performance. A *collaboration technique* is a reusable procedure for invoking useful interactions among people working toward a group goal (de Vreede et al., 2006).

Consider, as an example, research on ideation techniques. Osborn (1963) proposed the brainstorming technique as a way to invoke synergy, and so to improve the number and quality of ideas produced by groups. Several subsequent studies reported that groups following Osborn's technique do not outperform those using nominal group technique (Diehl & Stroebe 1987). Losses from production blocking, free-riding (social loafing), and evaluation apprehension appeared to outweigh possible benefits from synergy (Collaros & Anderson, 1969; Diehl & Stroebe 1987). Groups using electronic brainstorming techniques however, were shown to outperform both manual and nominal teams (Connolly et al., 1990; Dennis et al., 1990; Fjermestad & Hiltz, 1999; Gallupe et al., 1992).

Techniques that allow group members to interact anonymously appear to reduce evaluation apprehension (Connolly et al., 1990; Valacich et al., 1992) but may encourage social loafing (Harkins & Jackson, 1985; Paulus & Dzindolet, 1993; Sanna, 1992). Further, social comparison has been shown to reduce social loafing (Shepherd et al., 1996). Techniques that incorporate a devil's advocate role appear to foster creativity (Schulz-Hardt et al., 2008) and improve idea quality (Schweiger et al., 1986), yet they may reduce collaboration process satisfaction (Schweiger et al,. 1986; Valacich & Schwenk, 1995). Techniques that decompose the problem space and/or solution space also appear to increase brainstorming performance (Dennis et al., 1997; Santanen et al., 2004). There are similar bodies of literature surrounding techniques for other patterns of collaboration, for team building, and for other aspects of collaboration. Research suggests that different techniques impose different level of cognitive load on group leaders and members (Kolfschoten et al., 2007; Kolfschoten et al., 2009), and different collaboration techniques may require different levels of facilitation and technology skills (Kolfschoten et al., 2009).

Researchers have begun to collect and codify collaboration techniques as design pattern languages for various aspects of collaboration (e.g. Aalst et al., 2003; de Vreede et al. 2006; Khazanchi & Zigurs, 2006). A design pattern *"describes a problem which occurs over and over again and then describes the core of the solution to that problem, in such a way that you can use this solution a million times over, without ever doing it the same way twice"* (Alexander et al., 1977, p. x). Collaboration Engineering researchers have developed design patterns called thinkLets (de Vreede et al. 2006; de Vreede et al. 2009; Kolfschoten et al. 2006). ThinkLets are named, scripted collaboration technique for predictably and repeatedly invoking known patterns of collaboration among people working together toward a goal (de Vreede et al. 2009). They enable rapid development of coherent, multi-layered collaboration processes that may improve the productivity and quality of work life for teams (de Vreede et al. 2006). ThinkLets will be described in greater depth in the next chapter as they are a collection of best practices that a facilitator can use to elicit the aforementioned patterns of collaboration. From the research on collaboration techniques and pattern languages, Briggs et al. (2009) generalize an area of concern that they labeled "Techniques".

Deductive Validation of the Techniques Layer. Techniques are used to invoke patterns of collaboration. Until patterns of collaboration have been selected, it would not be possible to select techniques to invoke them. Concerns about techniques are therefore subordinate to concerns about patterns of collaboration. If a group changes the patterns of collaboration it wants to use to move through its activities, then it will have to change the techniques it uses, because techniques invoke patterns of collaboration. Techniques are therefore dependent on patterns of collaboration. A group may choose to change the technique it uses to invoke a particular pattern of collaboration. Patterns of collaboration are therefore independent of techniques. Lacking techniques, it would not be possible to select tools for implementing a technique, because each technique requires specific capabilities, nor would it be possible to prepare a script describing how the technique is to be instantiated. The Techniques layer must therefore fall below the Patterns of Collaboration layer, but above the Tools and Scripts layers of the SLMC.

The Tools Layer

Key Concerns for Facilitators. A great deal of research has been done about the design (Reinig, Briggs, & Nunamaker, 2007; Cataldo et al., 2006), deployment (Agres, de Vreede, & Briggs, 2005), and use (Golder & Huberman 2006; Kamrani & Abouel Nasr, 2008; Smith, 2007) of tools to support collaboration. Collaboration *tools* are instruments or apparatus used in performing an operation for moving a group toward its goals, for example, whiteboards, flipcharts, or collaboration software systems. Collaboration tools must afford users with the capabilities they require to execute their work. The collaboration technology market is burgeoning with new products appearing monthly. A number of authors have proposed schemes for making sense of the range of capabilities offered in the collaboration space (Bos et al., 2007; Mittleman et al., 2009; Penichet et al., 2007; Sahni, Van den Bergh, & Coninx, 2008). Researchers have developed and published a pattern language of design considerations for collaboration software. This work addresses ninety-seven generalized solutions for a range of functions such as community membership, workspace creation, shared artifacts, multi-modal communication, awareness, access control, persistence, and identification (Schummer & Lukosch, 2007).

Researchers have produced hundreds of articles on the use of group support systems (GSS) to improve group productivity (see Fjermestad & Hiltz 1998, 2000; Pervan & Arnott 2006) for thorough compendia of these works). These studies have addressed a broad set of topics such as anonymity (Valacich et al., 1992), group size (Gallupe et al., 1992), task type, task-technology fit (Zigurs &

Buckland, 1998), and national culture (DeSanctis & Gallupe, 1987; Watson, Ho, & Raman, 1994). Other researchers report on a variety of phenomena pertaining to, for example, wikis (Ebersbach et al., 2008), audio and video conferencing (Nguyen & Canny, 2007), and metaverses (e.g. virtual worlds like Second Life) (Davis et al., 2009), reporting ways that collaboration technology use can improve or impede group performance. From this literature, we derive an area of concern we label, "Tools." Briggs et al. (2009) choose the term, "Tools" over the term "technologies" because they contend that both computer-based and non-computer-based tools be included in this area of concern.

Deductive Validation of the Tools Layer. Tools afford the capabilities required to instantiate a collaboration technique. Until techniques have been selected, it would not be possible to select tools for instantiating the technique because each technique requires specific capabilities. Concerns about tools must therefore be subordinate to concerns about techniques. If a group changes the techniques it intends to use, it may need to change its tools, because the new techniques may require different capabilities. Tools are therefore dependent on techniques. A group may decide to use different tools to provide the capabilities their technique requires. Techniques are therefore independent of tools. Lacking tools, it would not be possible to create a script, because scripts provide guidance on how to use tools. The Tools layer must therefore fall below the Techniques layer, but above the Scripts layer in the SMLC.

The Scripts Layer

Key Concerns for Facilitators. A number of studies in the collaboration science arena address the scripts people use to move a group toward its goal. A *script* is everything team members say to other and do with their tools to move toward the group goal. An unstructured script would be description of emergent actions and utterances. A structured script would provide team members with procedural guidance (Kollar, Fischer, & Slotta, 2005), structuring and sequencing what participants in various roles should say and do to move the group forward (Kollar, Fischer, & Hesse, 2006). Internal scripts are procedural knowledge embedded in the cognitive schema of individuals (Abelson, 1981). External scripts are procedural guidance that is not necessarily integrated into the cognitive schemas of group members (Kollar, Fischer, & Slotta, 2005).

Structured external scripts for a group are often derived from collaboration techniques. In the thinkLets design pattern language, the essence of each technique is embodied as highly structured set of rules that specify a *sequence* of *actions* people in specific *roles* should take using certain *capabilities* under certain *constraints* (Kolfschoten et al., 2006). Each thinkLet includes a generic script that instantiates those rules. Designers of collaboration systems can tailor the thinkLet script or replace it completely, yet still invoke the same patterns of collaboration, so long as the new script still invokes the rules of the thinkLet (Kolfschoten et al., 2006). Facilitators' use of scripts in thinkLet-based collaborative problem solving will be further addressed in the next chapter.

Subtle variations in scripts can produce substantial variations in group performance. Simply instructing a brainstorming group to think creatively significantly increases the number of creative ideas they produce (Runco, Illies, & Reiter-Palmon, 2005). Instructing the group to engage in problem construction before brainstorming begins also increases their creativity (Reiter-Palmon et al., 1997). Shepherd, et al, (1996) reported that adding an invocation of social comparison to a brainstorming script increased the number of ideas produced by an anonymous brainstorming group by about 30%. For example group members might be told that "An average group produces about *xxx* ideas during a session like this. If you produce fewer, you are below average".

Figure 1. The Seven Layer Model of Collaboration. Each layer deals with different collaboration concerns for the designer of collaboration systems. Each has different phenomena of interest, and therefore different methods for modeling and measuring collaboration.

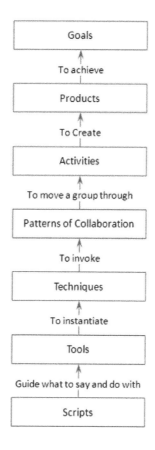

Furthermore, Shepherd et al. found that if the invocation were delivered in a jocular tone to increase its salience (e.g. "…If you produce less than that, you are brain-dead.") productivity increased by another 30%. Other research showed that varying the order of 20 prompts covering five topics in a directed brainstorming technique could yield variations of as high as 300% in the number of creative ideas a group produced (Santanen, Briggs, & de Vreede, 2000). Similar findings across a variety of domains demonstrate the value and importance of scripts to collaboration success. From this body of literature, Briggs et al. (2009) derived an area of concern that they labeled, "Scripts".

Deductive Validation of the Scripts Layer. Scripts provide guidance about the things people in various roles should do and say with their tools to instantiate the techniques selected for the group. Until tools have been selected, it would not be possible to prepare a script describing how to use them. Concerns about scripts must therefore be subordinate to concerns about Tools. If a group changes the tools it uses, then it must change its script to describe how to use the new tools. Scripts therefore depend on tools. A group may decide to use a different way of describing how tools should be used. Tools are therefore independent of scripts. The Scripts layer must therefore fall below the Tools layer in the SMLC

Interface between Layers

In addition to the concerns for each of the seven layers in the SLMC, there are concerns at the interfaces between each layer and the layer above it (Briggs et al., 2009). Between the Products and Goals Layer, one must consider the degree to which products are valuable toward goal attainment. Because goals vary from group to group, there are no universal measures of product value; such measures must be derived on a task-by-task basis. It may be possible, however, to derive general measures of the *perceived* value of products, with questions like, "The outcomes of today's efforts will (advance / inhibit) the achievement of our goals." Likewise, between the Goals and Activities Layers, a designer must take into account the degree to which activities create products that serve group goals. The purpose of the six patterns of collaboration is to provide a logical understanding of how a group will move through the activities it must complete in order to create its products. Of interest between the Activities and Patterns layers, therefore, is the effectiveness and efficiency with which the designed sequence of collaboration patterns would move a group through its activities to their interim goals and products. The purpose of techniques is to invoke patterns of collaboration that will be useful for moving a group through its activities. Of concern at the interface between the Techniques and Patterns layers, therefore, would be the degree to which each technique invokes the requisite patterns. Between the Tools and Techniques layers, a designer must consider the degree to which a given technology affords required capabilities, and the degree to which those capabilities are afforded at a minimum of financial, political, social, cognitive, emotional, and physical cost. Of interest between the Tools and Scripts layer would be the degree to which the scripts lead the group to use their tools in ways that faithfully invoke the technique chosen by the work practice designer.

Summary and Linkages of SLMC to Subsequent Chapters

Understanding, designing, and executing collaboration is a tall task for a facilitator, as the complexity of collaboration alone induces great cognitive load. The SLMC abstracts the why, what, and how of effective team collaboration into seven categories for facilitators collaborative processes and designers of collaborative systems. "*This separation of concerns (layers of collaboration) may reduce cognitive load for designers (of collaborative processes) and may help improve completeness and consistency of their designs, yielding higher productivity for collaborating groups*" (Briggs et al., 2009).

The SLMC integrates a vast body of theory and research from multiple disciplines into easy –to- understand foundations of effective collaboration. With the understanding that changes to one layer require adaptations to each lower layer, but may not necessitate changes to higher layers, designing effective collaboration is greatly simplified for moderately experienced collaboration designers. The chapter on *thinkLets* will explain how a collection of best practices in collaborative problem solving – thinkLets – utilizes specific combinations of collaboration layers. Further, the thinkLets chapter explains these layers and their interactive effects in greater detail. The chapter on collaboration technology will explain how SLMC provides a road map for maximizing the effectiveness of facilitated collaboration effectiveness via supportive collaboration technologies. Finally, the Collaboration Engineering chapter emphasizes how SLMC provides a framework for choices that must be made when designing collaborative problem solving efforts, and how SLMC can be used to dissect current collaboration designs.

Chapter Three

Facilitation

Why is Facilitation Important?

In offices all around the world, large amounts of time are spent in meetings. In Holland, annunal meetings cost on average $5000 per employee and approximentaly $37 billion a year is lost on poor meeting results (de Vreede, 2010). Not only board members, but leaders and managers, middle management, developers, interns and students spend precious time getting together to solve problems and explore opportunities. Usually people gather in one room to discuss an issue, but they can also be in different locations around the country or globe using technology. There are many kinds of meetings, but the basics are still the same. The people need to communicate and the communication needs some kind of structure to work effectively.

Most people accostumed to meetings have a story or two to describe how to waste a lot of time trying to collaborate. Often things start as a discussion to solve a problem, but end in chaos as the loudest people in the room try to promote their own solution without taking the time to evaluate the other participants' ideas.

Usually there is someone chairing the meeting. This person frequently calls the meeting and has a strong opinion on the topic. During the meeting, chairpersons are known for sticking to their agendas and controling the room any way he or she would like – as they tend to be authority figures. Also, the chairperson might not possess the necessary skills needed to assist people in a collaborative setting. Alternatively, when there is no agenda and/or the chairperson does not manage interpersonal interactions, other problems may arise, such as controversy about how to complete a task, or an overabundance of ideas may be generated (i.e., the group may not know how to choose what ideas to use).

Ineffectiveness occurs for numerous reasons. People may not express their honest opinions for fear of seeming in disagreement with their boss who is chairing the meeting, or for fear of asking dumb questions. Also, people aren't always that good at communicating with each other. When this happens, not only does the business lose money, but they might also make wrong managerial decisions as a result of bad communication.

When things spiral out-of-hand it's difficult to obtain a valuable outcome from a meeting. This occurrence often results in another meeting to follow-up on the same problem, as well as new problem that arose from the previous meeting. Therefore, time and money is lost because the organization has to double the amount of man-hours spent on one topic as a result of an ineffective initial meeting.

The answer to this cyclical and dynamic problem is facilitated collaborative problem solving. Facilitation – by definition – is a dynamic process that involves managing relationships between people, tasks, and technology, as well as structuring tasks and contributing to effective accomplishment of the meeting's outcome (de Vreede, 2002). Consquently, facilitation enables groups to work efficiently, effectively, and cooperatively toward a common goal. Facilitation can result in better and faster problem solving, organizational progess, and monetary and time benefits.

The purpose of this chapter is to address how facilitation of collaborative problem solving can be targeted to improve group decision making by means of following the Seven Layer Model of Collaboration (SLMC). As discussed in Chapter Two, the fourth layer the SLMC – principles of collaboration – consists of six main patterns of collaboration: generate, reduce, clarify, organize, evaluate, and build consensus. When combined and implemented appropriately by a facilitator, these patterns of collaboration help groups make efficient, high quality decisions. Specifically, this chapter explains how the best practices in collaboration science, such as the aforementioned patterns of collaboration, can be properly aligned and implemented by facilitators using thinkLets. ThinkLets – a collection of optimal facilitation techniques – will be discussed in the next chapter.

What is Facilitation?

The literature on facilitation can be divided into three non-mutually exclusive parts (de Vreede, Niederman, & Paarlberg, 2002). Some studies examine the functions and tasks of a facilitator, while others investigate the effect that a facilitator has on the meeting and its outcomes. Finally, a few research efforts have addressed facilitation from the perspective of the participants of a meeting. Notably, a distinction also exists between 'technical' and 'group process'. For purposes of this book we only address group process facilitation because it involves monitoring interpersonal interactions and task accomplishment; whereas, technical facilitation is solely aimed at helping participants with use technology associated with collaboration.

Facilitation Tasks, Functions, and Characteristics

Facilitation tasks may focus on meeting *process* or meeting *content*. Process facilitation provides structure and general support to groups during the meeting. It involves ensuring that an equality of participation is achieved, blind alleys are not overtly explored, and time is managed appropriately (de Vreede, Boonstra, & Niederman, 2002). Content facilitation focuses on the content of the meeting, analyzing the data, and displaying relevant issues. With content facilitation the facilitator gives more information or direction than the impartial information or direction provided with process facilitation. While some argue that facilitators should not make content contributions, others maintain that content and process facilitation are not exclusive and should inform each other to achieve a multiplier effect.

Dickson et al. (1996) distinguish between two types of process facilitation: 'task interventions', meant to focus the group's attention on the task, and 'interactional interventions', aimed at the participants and their relations. The tasks of a facilitator with these two types of interventions differ significantly (see Table 1). Other authors do not make a difference between task and interactional interventions.

Table 1: Facilitation Task Types (adapted from de Vreede et al., 2002)

Task Interventions	Interactional Interventions
•Structures group activities • Guides the agenda • Clarifies and rephrases issues • Keeps discussions on topic • Reformulates questions or problems • Summarizes • Tests agreements among participants • Identifies decisions	• Equalizes participation of participants • Identifies communication problems • Solicits feedback • Manages conflict • Provides and aids the group's emotional climate

Clawson and Bostrom collected information from experienced GSS facilitators about their most important tasks and categorized the feedback into sixteen facilitation dimensions. These dimensions show the qualities a facilitator must have and the functions (s)he must execute during a meeting (see Table 2). Not only functions, but also skills and qualities of character are believed to be an important factor in being successful at helping groups to achieve their goals.

Table 2: Facilitation Functions and Qualities (adapted from de Vreede et al., 2002)

1. Plans and designs the meeting 2. Listens to, clarifies and integrates information 3. Demonstrates flexibility 4. Keeps group outcome focused 5. Creates and reinforces an open, positive and 6. Selects and prepares appropriate technology participative environment 7. Directs and manages the meeting 8. Develops and asks the right questions 9. Promotes ownership and encourages group 10. Actively builds rapport and relationships responsibility 11. Demonstrates self-awareness and self-	expression 12. Manages conflict and negative emotions constructively 13. Encourages/supports multiple perspectives 14. Understands technology and its capabilities 15. Creates comfort with and promotes understanding of the 16. Presents information to group technology and technology outputs

Niederman et al. (1996) interviewed 37 facilitators with different GSS experience. From these interviews a number of required qualities of character came forth (see Table 3). The importance of these qualities was perceived differently between experienced and non-experienced facilitators. More experienced facilitators considered 'flexibility' important. This may be due to some insecurity of non-experienced facilitators about the reliability of the GSS technology. The most important qualities appeared to be 'good communication skills' and 'ego-less facilitation'.

Table 3: Facilitator Skills and Qualities (adapted from de Vreede et al., 2002)	
Good communication skills Ego-less facilitation Flexibility	Task focus Understanding the group and its objectives Leadership

Facilitation Effects on Meetings and Outcomes

Research indicates that facilitation tends to have a positive effect on participant consensus and satisfaction (as reported by the facilitator). For instance, Anson et al. (1995) found that facilitation enhanced group processes, cohesion, and outcomes for both GSS-supported and non-supported groups. More specifically, Miranda and Bostrom (1999) found that process facilitation had a positive effect on both meeting process and participant satisfaction, regardless of GSS support. Conversely, they discovered that content facilitation had a negative influence, unless it was supported by GSS. The benefits of technology-based facilitation are discussed later in the next chapter.

Participant Perceptions of Facilitation

In most collaboration studies, facilitators themselves were the source of information on what they do and how effectively they achieved desired results. Three studies have yielded particularly interesting results regarding participants' perceptions of facilitation. One early study conducted by Ackermann (1996) indicated that participants could identify important tasks to be conducted before, during, and after facilitation sessions. De Vreede, Niederman, & Paarlberg (2002) found that when participants' perceptions from 34 GSS meetings were assessed, three distinct facilitation dimensions – salient to participants – were identified and positively related to participant satisfaction: 1) atmosphere management and meeting design; 2) content focus; and 3) technology and professionalism. Furthermore, a study conducted by de Vreede, Boonstra, & Niederman (2002) revealed that 250 interviewee statements regarding *what facilitators should do to be effective* could be placed in at least 1 or 12 categories (see Table 4). These 12 categories represent a comprehensive framework of what participants perceive to be essential to the effectiveness of GSS facilitators.

Table 4. Twelve Category Framework of Effective Facilitation, as Described by Participants (Adapted from de Vreede, Boonstra, & Niederman, 2002).

A. Workshop design. The facilitator should prepare the meeting, carefully taking aspects such as the meeting objective, the timeline, the topic, and the critical issues into account. Also, the facilitator should choose and prepare adequate meeting accommodation.

B. Required knowledge. The facilitator should have substantial knowledge and experience on the GSS instruments, the meeting topic, and group processes & group dynamics.

C. Setting the stage. At the beginning of the meeting, the facilitator should give a clear and understandable introduction, including an introduction to the meeting process and its rules, on the GSS technology and its possibilities, and on the meeting topic.

D. Being available. The facilitator has to be available for questions, explanations etc. throughout the meeting.

E. Human qualities and attributes. A facilitator should balance between appearing relaxed, neutral and a little reserved and being in charge of the meeting, being somewhat charismatic and spontaneous. Also, a facilitator should possess a number of basic social skills such as being able to listen and communicate.

F. Being sensitive / building rapport. During the meeting, the facilitator should interact with the problem owner and consult him on a number of issues such as the meeting progress and the discussion content. Also, the facilitator should make sure that all participants can participate in a meaningful, significant and equal way. (S)he should easily interact with the group and be broadly accepted.

G. Intermediate results / group output presentation. The facilitator should arrange and/or give summaries and/or feedback during & after the meeting, and be able to identify interesting contributions from less interesting ones.

H. Directing
- *Meeting process.* The facilitator should motivate and stimulate the group to preserve a productive and constructive environment during the meeting. Also, (s)he should be able to tighten the reins or give free rein if the situation calls for it.
- *Group toward output/results.* The facilitator should make sure that the group achieves its goals and guard a balance between results and time. Also, the facilitator should lead and direct the group making sure that results-oriented discussions start and continue.

I. Guarding. The facilitator should guard the discussion focus, directing the discussions to the main issues in a determined yet acceptable manner. The facilitator should keep track of time but not break off activities too soon.

J. Script evaluation/modification and redesigning process. The facilitator should structure the oral as well as the electronic discussion and show the flexibility to adapt the script or meeting process to 'hot issues' or an unexpected turn in the discussion.

K. Being sensitive to results. The facilitator should monitor and understand the electronic discussion and the subject(s) treated, (s)he should analyze the output and be able to quickly distil trends from participants' contributions. The facilitator should handle the contributions respectfully.

L. After-care. The facilitator should interpret the meeting outcomes.

The Role of the Facilitator

A facilitator is someone who uses some level of intuition or explicit knowledge of group processes to formulate and deliver some form of formal or informal process interventions at a shallow or deep level to help a group achieve a common goal (de Vreede et al., 2003). A facilitator is responsible for the participation, structuring, and simplification of group interaction and collaboration in pursuit of a common goal. In doing so, they draw from arsenal of collaboration techniques to design and execute productive work practices on behalf of the teams they serve. A facilitator also plays the role of an impartial moderator of group processes and typically has excellent communication and interpersonal skills. Further, there are four primary functions of facilitators that make them particularly effective in group meetings: process guide, tool giver, neutral third-party, and process educator (Straus, 2002).

Process guide. There are always two parts to a conversation: the process (i.e., how people interact) and the content (i.e., the subject(s) of conversation). It's almost impossible for a single person to lead and manage both of these aspects of a conversation at the same time. This is where the role of the facilitator comes into action. If a manager or leader of an organization tries to lead a meeting where a discussion is at hand, or a goal is being pursued, the meeting discussion could be biased in favor of the leader. Thus, when a facilitator is brought in on a meeting the manager/leader does not have to lead the discussion, and can partake in the decision making process without manipulating the final decision points (Straus, 2002). In simple text, the facilitator is a process guide who does not contribute to the discussion of group ideas; they simply listen and keep the group on task. The facilitator is not a group leader per se, as (s)he offers process suggestions, enforces rules, addresses conflict, and ensures everyone participates.

Tool giver. A facilitator should possess knowledge of decision making methods and problem-solving skills. Facilitators should be able to transfer this knowledge to the group when appropriate so that facilitators provide can provide collaboration tools to the group. This tool giver function follows the philosophy of teaching a man to fish (learn a process), rather than giving him a fish (a single idea). Straus (2002) suggests that when a facilitator teaches a group how to resolve a problem the group avoids multi-headed animal syndrome – everyone tries to head-off in a different direction but cannot go their way because the other body parts (group members) each want to go somewhere else.

Neutral third-party. The third function of a facilitator is self-explanatory in regard to the title: neutral third-party. The facilitator has to come into the meeting with an open-mind and no biases. It's not that the facilitators will not have input on the matter-at-hand or their own opinions; rather, it is the job of facilitators to be a neutral, unbiased third party who guides the decision making process to be as productive as possible. Additionally, a facilitator does not have to be an external employee in order to be a third-party. An unbiased third party could be employed by the organization with the problem so long as the facilitator is not familiar with the group members and problem at-hand. However, the advantage of using an external facilitator is that no participants will question their inherent biases.

Process educator. The final function of the facilitator – process education – requires teaching the group what steps they are taking to achieve their common goal. Through excellent teaching of effective group processes, the need for the facilitator should be lessened. However, the challenge of this function is to teach group processes without taking too much extra time to achieve the group objectives. One way a facilitator can be a successful process educator at a decisive strategic moment is to say "OK, we have just finished brainstorming a list of ideas. We are at a strategic moment. We have several choices as to how to proceed with organizing this list. One thing we can do is review the list and clarify ideas that you don't understand. Or, we could first eliminate ideas that are redundant. I would recommend that you begin by clarifying first so that you are certain of understanding each item before you merge or remove ideas.

Chapter Four

ThinkLets

Why use thinkLets?

How do facilitators integrate the SLCM and the role of the facilitator such that collaboration challenges are minimized and the benefits of collaboration technology are maximized? If the facilitator manages to design an effective decision making process, how does the facilitator simultaneously monitor and guide interpersonal interactions, participation, and information flow? With all of the details to consider, skills to obtain, and technology to configure when facilitating high quality collaboration, how can an organization afford to hire external facilitators every time a team decision needs to be made?

Utilize thinkLets! ThinkLets are proven facilitation techniques that can be used to optimize collaborative problem solving. ThinkLets allows an amateur facilitator to easily design and implement collaboration processes tailored to the needs of a problem owner. ThinkLets simplify the functions of the SLCM, specifically capitalizing on the patterns of collaboration discussed within the fourth layer of the model. Importantly, thinkLets are designed for ease of use with GSS and each thinkLet has instructions for how to appropriately configure GSS during each problem solving stage.

What is a thinkLet?

A thinkLet is a single "reusable, predictable and transferable *facilitation technique* that can be used to move a group through a process towards it agreed goal" (de Vreede, Kolfschoten, & Briggs, 2006, p. 142). A thinkLet summarizes the *best practice* in regards to a collaboration activity that a facilitator can utilize to evoke a certain pattern of group behavior by means of giving short and simple instructions to the group (Briggs & de Vreede, 2009; Briggs, de Vreede, & Nunamaker, 2003). For instance, some thinkLets are designed to yield a wide variety of ideas by means of requiring group members to generate as much information as possible without evaluating it. In this case, the process of generating ideas is separate from the process of evaluating information because group members can focus their attention on a single task that is uninterrupted by interpersonal discussion.

When thinkLets are appropriately combined, they guide group members through a reasoning process that involves a sequence of collaboration patterns that allow members to focus all of their attention on a singular, more manageable reasoning task (Briggs & de Vreede, 2009). Certain thinkLets work better in combination than others. How to decide what thinkLets should be paired together is discussed later in the chapter. The main take-away point here is that thinkLets are building blocks (i.e., collaborative decision making activities) for eliciting specific group behavior at each stage of a well-structured collaborative reasoning process (Briggs & de Vreede, 2009; de Vreede et al., 2006;

Kolfschoten & de Vreede, 2007). Hence, it is the successful integration of multiple thinkLets into a collaborative decision making process – more so than the utility of any single thinkLet activity – that drives the development of faster, higher quality group decisions.

ThinkLet Components

Importantly, thinkLets are documented according to a specific template that always includes a name, script, tool, and configuration (Briggs & de Vreede, 2009). It is the specification and combination of the three latter template components that act as the stimulus for the collaboration pattern targeted by a thinkLet (Briggs et al., 2003). Precision, consistency, and simplicity in thinkLet documentation are necessary to ensure predictability and repeatability of group behavior and outcomes. If the logic or instructions between the administrations of two thinkLets differs, it is likely that groups will react differently to each thinkLet.

Name

The first component of a thinkLet template – its name – makes the facilitation technique easy to remember by providing an identity that is metaphorically related to the coinciding collaboration process (Kolfschoten & de Vreede, 2007). The thinkLet name is intended to be catchy and serve as mnemonic that will support recognition and memorization of the thinkLet. Also, a picture or icon that is metaphorically related to the thinkLet name usually accompanies the thinkLet description. Along with these identifiers, a brief overview of the steps involved in executing the thinkLet is included.

Script

The second primary component of a thinkLet is the script. A thinkLet script provides the facilitator with a sequence of things to do and say, which is intended to evoke the pattern of collaboration targeted by the thinkLet (Briggs & de Vreede, 2009; Kolfschoten & de Vreede, 2007). Holding everything else equal, thinkLets that differ even slightly in the wording of their respective scripts can yield different group behavior. For instance, Shepherd, Briggs, Reinig, and Nunamaker (1997) found that when assessing the effects of social comparison on brainstorming productivity, participants who received social comparisons that were made in a more jocular tone, such as that person "kicked butt" – as opposed to "had above average performance" – were more productive at brainstorming.

The rules set forth in the script are at the heart of what makes a thinkLet effective. Rules communicated from the script have one of two purposes: 1) to evoke action from group members; or 2) to adjust actions of participants (Kolfschoten & de Vreede, 2007). The former rule – referred to as an *instruction intervention* – describes who should do what, which tools should be used, and which constraints should apply. The latter rule – an *adjustment intervention* – specifies when (i.e., under what circumstance) an intervention is necessary, and what changes that entails.

Tool

The third major component of a thinkLet is the tool used to collect, transfer, and display information resulting from collaboration (Briggs & de Vreede, 2009; Briggs et al., 2003). A thinkLet tool is defined as "the specific version of the specific hardware and software technology used to create a pattern of thinking" (Kolfschoten & de Vreede, 2009, p. 2). Thus, a technology designed to facilitate collaborative problem solving, such as Group Support Systems (GSS) mentioned in Chapter 4, utilizes different decision making activities to elicit certain patterns of collaboration (Briggs et al., 2003). For example, a brainstorming activity yields different behavior and outcomes than an idea evaluation activity like voting on the best problem solution. Further, different software (e.g., GSS vs. ThinkTank) may yield different patterns of collaboration in response to the same type of activity. For instance, a brainstorming activity in one computer program may allow all participants to compile their ideas on a single communal list simultaneously viewed by everyone; whereas another program may require participants to put some ideas on one of many lists, and then swap lists with another member. Research indicates that such seemingly small differences in how an activity is administered can make a considerable difference in the outcome of the thinkLet (Dennis et al., 1997; Easton, George, Nunamaker, & Pendergast, 1990; Hollingshead, McGrath, & O'Connor, 1993). Further, facilitating collaborative problem solving via a whiteboard or paper and pencil can be quite different than administering the process electronically. The differences between electronic versus manual application of thinkLets are discussed later in the chapter.

Tool Configuration

The fourth and final component of a thinkLet is the configuration of the tool used to administer the thinkLet. ThinkLet tool configuration refers to the user options and limitations participants are allowed to operate within when partaking in a collaboration activity (Briggs et al., 2006). For example, the brainstorming activity in GSS has the option to allow anonymous submission of group member ideas. Configuring the brainstorming tool in this manner is likely to alter the collaboration process because group members do not have to fear being judged by others, and the quality of an idea should be judged more so than the credibility of who submitted it. When a manual tool is used, configurations are usually physical limitations imposed on the materials, such as the number of stickies circulated amongst the group.

Documentation

Furthermore, thinkLet documentation usually includes additional information that aids the facilitator in recognition, design, understanding, and execution of each thinkLet (Kolfschoten & de Vreede, 2007). From the standpoint of a facilitator, it is particularly useful to document *what is expected to happen as a result of executing a thinkLet*. In doing so the anticipated behavior of group members should be specified, as well as what challenges might transpire, how long will the thinkLet take, and what results are hypothesized. Additionally, facilitators need to collect information on whether and how their thinkLet design can be supported. This documentation is referred to as *selection guidance*, which entails identification of what pattern of collaboration the thinkLet facilitates, what modifications can be made to create variations of the thinkLet, and how the results of the process should be classified.

Example of Actual thinkLets Components.

Adapted from *ThinkLets: Building Blocks for Concerted Collaboration* (Briggs & de Vreede, 2009).

Name: FastFocus
Script: *Say this:* "Read through the brainstorming ideas on the screen in front of you and for [important ideas]". *Do this:* Write each new idea on a public list. *Say this if a proposed idea is already on the list:* How is your idea different from [idea x] on the list? *Do this:* When all participants have had a turn, tell everybody to swap pages; start a second round. For the third round, ask the whole group if anyone has an [important idea] that is not on the list. Repeat until no one wants to add anything new to the list.
Tool: ThinkTank or GroupSystems
Tool configuration: 1. Participants view their comments/ideas in the Electronic Brainstorming screen; 2. The facilitator displays an empty list (e.g., in Vote or Categorizer screen). 3. Make participant contributions anonymous.
Documentation: Elicit convergence, clarification, and reduction patterns of collaboration by ensuring all the ideas of concern in a category/grouping are discussed in regards to their strengths and/or weaknesses.

Why Are thinkLets Effective?

ThinkLets are expert facilitators' best practices for eliciting goal directed collaborative decision making because they are goal-centered, minimize cognitive load, and systematically reduce group work challenges (Briggs & de Vreede, 2009; Briggs et al., 2006; de Vreede et al., 2006; Kolfschoten & de Vreede, 2007). Additionally, they are easy to: learn, execute, align with one another, modify, remember, and transfer.

Advantages of thinkLets

Many of the advantages of thinkLets can be credited to the Alexandrian design pattern language that defines their structural template. Alexander (1979) identified his architectural design patterns as reusable solutions that could be applied to frequently occurring architectural problems. He suggested that "a pattern describes a problem which occurs over and over again and then describes the core of the solution to that problem in such a way that you can use this solution a million times over, without ever doing it the same way twice" (Alexander et al., 1977, p. 10; as cited in de Vreede et al., 2006). Similarly, thinkLets are applied to recurring situations and yield predictable, repeatable outcomes by means of implementing the same core activities that can be modified without substantially changing the nature of the thinkLet. Alexander identified several advantages of utilizing pattern design and language that are also capitalized on by thinkLets. Some of these advantages and how they are reflected by thinkLets are identified in de Vreede et al. (2006) and summarized below:

- *A pattern design language provides a convenient and common language for communication.* Facilitators and/or collaboration engineers can easily discuss and transfer a thinkLet process design back and forth using no more than a page or two of documentation (de Vreede & Briggs, 2005). This consistent and intuitive language allows clear and fast transmission of information regarding sophisticated collaboration processes.
- *New or improved patterns are easily inspired and implemented.* When the need for improvement in a collaboration activity is identified, a simple change in a thinkLet script, tool, or configuration can yield the necessary behavioral adjustment.
- *Larger systems can be designed based on individual patterns.* ThinkLets can be combined into reusable sub-processes that yield new or modified collaboration techniques, standard operating procedures for teams, and even organizational decision making procedures.

© The Center for Collaboration Science

- *Pattern design language makes it easy to teach, capture, and share expert design knowledge.* As previously discussed in regards to the naming and identification of thinkLets, the metaphorical description of thinkLets makes them easy to discuss and transfer. The thinkLet documentation process suggested by the thinkLets user guide can be completed in less than two pages (Briggs & de Vreede, 2009; Kolfschoten & de Vreede, 2007). Comprehensive and accurate description of a thinkLet's script, tool, and configuration typically provides enough information to successfully execute the desired collaboration process.

- *Anyone can create with patterns.* Research has shown that novice facilitators can successfully execute thinkLets-based processes after one-to-two days of training (de Vreede & Briggs, 2005). Further, the structure (e.g., script, tool, and configuration) of thinkLets makes it easy for anyone to understand how to create a thinkLet; however, very few practitioners understand group processes well enough to develop their own collaboration process.

- *Pattern designs can improve the quality of life.* Team and organizational productivity can be enhanced when thinkLets are utilized to make collaborative decisions. They can also improve the fairness of group decisions by means of concealing the identity of who contributes what information, and through voting to make final decisions. Also, participants are protected from personal attacks.

- *Pattern designs create coherent systems.* ThinkLets clearly fit this bill as they almost always work in combination with one another to yield a multifaceted group decision process. Further, each time a thinkLet-based process is utilized it should be tailored to the environment, team culture, agreed upon goal, and the activities that will precede and follow each thinkLet activity.

In addition to the pattern design nature of thinkLets, there are three primary aspects of a thinkLet-based reasoning process that alleviate many of the group process challenges identified in the first section of this chapter: 1) participants can anonymously contribute ideas; 2) participants can engage in the process simultaneously; and 3) the problem solving process is structured such that stages of decision making are focused, manageable, and do not conflict with other stages.

Anonymity

First, anonymity of idea contribution occurs when the group does not know who contributed what ideas. Anonymity of idea contributions can be applied to any thinkLet by means of selecting this option as part of the tool configuration. Notably, this configuration is not limited to electronic facilitation tools, which will be discussed in the final section of this chapter. Anonymity of idea contribution can enhance the effectiveness of a thinkLet for the following reasons:

- Evaluation apprehension is minimized

- Ideas and suggestions are judged based on quality and merit, NOT the contributing member's credibility or authority

- Interpersonal conflicts due to race, age, and personality differences are reduced (Vissers & Dankbaar, 2002)

Parallel/Simultaneous Workflow

Second, group effectiveness is increased when a thinkLet requires parallel or simultaneous workflow contributions from group members. Parallel workflow makes the group more efficient because participants do not have downtime – they are continually contributing information to the problem solving process instead of waiting for other members to discuss their ideas.

Advantages of Parallel/Simultaneous Workflow Contributions:

- Reduces production blocking because groups members do not have to wait their turn to contribute to the reasoning process (e.g., ideas can be generated, organized, or evaluated by each person at the same time)

    o "Automatic minutes" are gained as the group works simultaneously instead of taking turns sharing ideas

    o Eliminates the forgetting of ideas due to production blocking

    o Reduces cognitive load when participants do not have to waist attention resources storing information into memory while listening to other group members

    o When cognitive load is reduced, more effort can be put into critical thinking processes, thus improving the quality of individual contributions

Structuring thinkLets

Third, utilizing a collection of complementary thinkLets to make group decisions improves group effectiveness because each pattern of collaboration subsumed under a thinkLet is narrowly focused on a stage of the decision making process that should not overlap with other processes. For example, during a brainstorming activity, participants should not debate the usefulness of others' ideas because this takes their attention away from the idea generation process – which may reduce the number or quality of items generated by people spending their attention resources challenging someone else's idea(s). Additional reasons the structure of a thinkLet-based reasoning processing increases collaborative problem solving effectiveness are summarized below:

- Increases quality and originality of group solutions when:

    o The reasoning process balances convergent and divergent thinking, as discussed in the next section (Brown & Paulus, 2002; Litchfield, 2008)

    o Evaluation of ideas is delayed until the idea generation stage of problem solving is complete (Drach-Zehavy, & Somech; 2001; Hoegl, Weinkauf, & Gemueden, 2004)

    o Participants have a shared understanding of what the group knows (Drach-Zehavy, & Somech; 2001; Hoegl et al., 2004)

- Guides structured debate/evaluation of ideas that improves outcome quality because the strengths and weakness of ideas are highlighted

- Reduces relationship conflict when participants are not allowed to criticize one another

- Reduces *groupthink* when thinkLets allow open criticism of an idea

- Increases fairness, democracy, and objectivity when thinkLets restrict evaluation of an idea to an anonymous vote

Organizational Implementation of ThinkLets

Not only are thinkLets great tools for making collaborative decisions to solve a particular problem, they can be implemented into an organization for various group processes (Kolfschoten & de Vreede, 2007). Formally implementing ThinkLets into group processes is a proven tool for supporting mission critical tasks. For example, thinkLets can be used in a formal group process to support marketing focus groups or project evaluation sessions. Importantly, staff members can easily be trained to facilitate thinkLets-based processes and modify them as needed. Training staff members to become experts in a few thinkLets processes is much cheaper than hiring an expensive external facilitator.

Electronic Versus Manual thinkLet Tools

As previously discussed, thinkLets provide a repeatable process to achieve a desired outcome. The process is rule driven, but flexible enough that the medium for implementation, or the tool, can be chosen for different situations. We have examined what a thinkLet is, why thinkLets are useful, and how to choose the right thinkLet. The next step in conquering thinkLets is to understand how to choose the appropriate tool for implementation. ThinkLets are designed so that they can be easily implemented through a manual or an electronic process. This section will compare and contrast the use of manual versus electronic tools to implement thinkLets.

Manual Implementation of thinkLets

Manual tools to implement thinkLets include sticky notes, flip-overs, dry-erase boards, or even simple sheets of paper. The facilitator simply directs the participants to pass around sheets of paper for brainstorming, look at the flip-over for group activities, or write on a sticky note to mark their vote. There are many advantages and disadvantages to this method.

- Manual Benefits
    - Manual implementation is reliable. You just have to remember to bring the paper and pens.
    - Easy to be flexible and change implementation on the fly.
    - Great with groups that do not understand technology or have handicaps that make using technology difficult.

- o ALWAYS a feasible back-up in the event of electronic failure. Notably, the same thinkLets can be implemented manually as electronically; however, when dealing with a large group, individuals may need to be paired into small teams.

- Manual Detriments

  - o Hard to manually calculate and view the results and trends quickly.

  - o More difficult to facilitate anonymity and parallel communication in comparison to electronic sessions because the facilitator must continually manipulate the flow of information by hand.

  - o Legibility of participants' writing can be poor, thus forcing authors to identify themselves if they wish to clarify their ideas.

  - o Time and space due to set-up of paper templates is more intensive.

Although it is much easier to click a button to ensure anonymity in electronic facilitation sessions, paper and pencil techniques can also protect idea anonymity. Typically, this is achieved by having the facilitator collect participant contributions, and then redistribute the contributions such that participants do not know who had access to the information they are viewing. For example, the facilitator could keep brainstorming contributions anonymous by giving everyone their own piece of paper to record a single idea for solving a problem, and instruct them to give him their paper when they are done. He could keep the papers out-of-sight when they are collected and redistribute them to a new person without revealing who had the paper last – instructing them to record their next best solution. Typically, a facilitator using this method would hold two more pieces of paper than there are group members so each time a single paper is returned, it can be redistributed without group members knowing it came from the last person to submit a paper.

In contrast to manual facilitation tools, electronic tools utilize the support of computer technology – most commonly GSS – to support thinkLet-based collaboration sessions. There are several software solutions available and they each have their own advantages and disadvantages.

- Electronic Benefits

  - o Provides a structure and concrete agenda that can be easily viewed and followed on a projector or computer screen such that changes can be viewed immediately by all participants.

  - o Requires additional facilitator preparation that instills greater confidence.

- o Helps facilitate anonymity and parallel communication.

  - o Provides greater data processing capacity so large amounts of information can be processed and transferred quickly.

  - o A session can be quickly put together anywhere there is an internet connect in the event that a group decision needs to be made in a hurry.

- Electronic Detriments

  - o Only so many facilitation software programs are available and not all are actively maintained.

  - o Facilitator must completely understand the technology and its limitations on top of understanding thinkLets and the group's dynamics.

  - o The software options may not be a perfect fit to completely follow each thinkLet.

  - o Software and technology is not always reliable.

Some thinkLets lend themselves to one tool better than others. The beauty of thinkLets is that they can be administered in either medium. It is important to understand how each thinkLet could be implemented both manually and electronically in case something goes wrong during the facilitation or preparation. It is also important to consider your group, the group dynamics, your comfort level with the tools, and the thinkLet itself when choosing your implementation strategy. The next chapter will explain GSS and other collaboration technologies in more detail.

Summary

ThinkLets have dramatically improved collaborative problem solving by means of minimizing social and cognitive challenges commonly associated with group work. They provide reusable, predictable, and transferable techniques for achieving group goals. Their simple instructions and pattern language basis make them easy to understand and use for novice and seasoned facilitators alike. ThinkLets are designed to support the collaborative process through six primary sub-patterns of collaboration: generate, clarify, reduce, organize, evaluate, and build consensus on ideas within a group. Not only do facilitators find thinkLets incredibly helpful when conducting isolated problem solving sessions, organizations can implement them on a routine basis when they are integrated into group processes and as a standard method for strategic decision making. Importantly, many different kinds of manual and electronic tools can be used to support thinkLets-based decision making processes.

Chapter Five

ThinkLets: Patterns of Collaboration

Designing a thinkLets Based Process

The Seven Layer Model of Collaboration provides a road map for how to design a thinkLet-based collaboration process (see Chapter Two). As illustrated in the SLMC, designing a thinkLets-based process, you must first determine the agreed goal of the problem solving effort, and then you must determine the sequence of thinkLets that is most likely to produce the desired results. Assuming the goal is established and everyone buys-in, you determine your thinkLet sequence by considering what combination of collaboration patterns is most useful. For each collaboration pattern selected, a sub-pattern of group deliberation that best aligns with your goal should be identified. Once a sub-pattern is identified, it is easy to know which thinkLet to use because you can match the collaboration sub-pattern to the process description of the appropriate thinkLet.

The aforementioned six patterns of collaboration listed in the fourth layer of the SLMC can be elicited by thinkLets, and they tend to be implemented in the following order: generate, reduce, clarify, organize, evaluate, and build consensus (Briggs et al., 2005; Kolfschoten & de Vreede, 2007). Sometimes multiple patterns of collaboration are subsumed under a single thinkLet. For example, some thinkLets, such as a BucketWalk, both reduce and clarify information. Moreover, a set of collaboration patterns may be repeated within a single process design. This commonly occurs when the goal of a facilitation session is to identify the cause(s) of a problem and determine how to alleviate those causes. Here, collaborative patterns such as generate – organize – reduce – clarify are likely needed to identify the causes of the problem, and then this same set of patterns will be needed to develop solutions to the core causes of the problem. Now that you understand the general framework of a thinkLets-based process, you must develop a thorough understanding of each collaboration pattern and how individual thinkLets instantiate it.

Generate

The generate pattern is typically the first stage of a problem solving effort, and its purpose is to create concepts that have not yet been considered (Brigg & de Vreede, 2009). This stage involves generating all possible information that should be considered when identifying or solving a problem. Thus, it increases the amount of information shared by the group by means of tapping the aggregate expertise, knowledge, and critical thinking skills of the group. The reason this collaboration kicks-off the problem solving process is that it allows individuals to focus on generating information – once cognitive resources are used to organize, reduce, clarify, and evaluate that information, it will become more difficult to generate new information. Further, these latter cognitive processes contaminate divergent thinking and begin to put restrictions on what ideas can be generated (Drach-Zehavy, & Somech; 2001; Hoegl et al., 2004). Therefore, it is important that participants understand that they are not to discuss, or personally evaluate ideas during the *generate* pattern because such behavior is likely to damage the quality, quantity, and originality of information the group has to work with.

There are three sub-patterns of collaboration subsumed under the generation pattern: *creativity*, *gathering*, and *reflecting* (Kolfschoten & de Vreede, 2007).

Creativity. A creativity sub-pattern aims to increase the gross number of concepts in the concept pool shared by the group. Creativity is enhanced by collecting the most diverse information possible and determining how it can be used to formulate the most unique, high quality idea possible (Mumford, Reiter-Palmon, & Redmond, 1994). Thus, the creativity sub-pattern is more likely to enhance group creativity with every new concept added to the idea pool. This is the sub-pattern you would utilize if the group goal was to produce a novel and useful solution, such as the theme of an edgy marketing campaign. The instructions for a thinkLet matching the creativity sub-pattern should be as unrestrictive as possible so that participants' thought processes are divergent and unconstrained.

Gathering and elaborating. The second sub-pattern, referred to as gathering or elaborating, purports to increase the completeness and relevance of information shared by the group (Kolfschoten & de Vreede, 2007). In this pattern, the amount of information generated is less important than the quality and applicability of the information. This pattern should be implemented if the agreed goal is to generate the highest quality solution. The thinkLet matched with the gathering sub-pattern should have a script that is somewhat more restrictive than a creativity script, as the ideas generated should be focused and on-point.

Reflecting. The third sub-pattern of the generation collaboration pattern is reflecting. Reflecting is the process of moving from less to more understanding of the relative value of concepts shared by the group (Kolfschoten & de Vreede, 2007). While this process entails information gathering, it is also a sub-pattern of evaluation. The reflecting sub-pattern is typically used to gather concept information from qualitative evaluations, reviews, and feedback sessions. This sub-pattern is particularly useful if the agreed goal is to assign relative value to a concept, problem, or potential solution. Relative values assigned to concepts are frequently used to make comparisons between concepts, such as the risk level of adding a new partner to a firm versus the benefits of the expansion.

Importantly, any of the three generate patterns can be started from scratch or started from seeds (Briggs & de Vreede, 2009). Starting from scratch indicates that the group aims to create concepts that have not yet been considered. Here, the FreeBrainstorm thinkLet is likely to be implemented and participants will be instructed to generate as many ideas as possible. Starting from seeds means that group members will be given a concept that already exists and then be assigned to expand upon it. When the goal is to analyze or elaborate upon a concept, seeds are necessary. A thinkLet that provides preconceived concepts and categories to cue potential ideas – such as a DirectedBrainstorm or LeafHopper – will be used to establish the starting blocks for seeded idea generation.

It is important to understand that when planning an idea generation activity, the more restrictive the instructions are when given to the participant, the more narrow their thinking (Mumford et al., 1994). Granted presenting participants with small amounts of information can cue divergent thinking, typically the more seeds or rules involved in the idea generation process the less creative group outcome. Hence, facilitators must be cognizant that minimal instructions for idea generation should be provided if creativity is a desired outcome. When deeper, more focused ideas are needed, providing cues such as categories of pertinent information tends to activate convergent thinking needed to develop solutions of the highest quality.

Reduce

The next two patterns of collaboration – reduce and clarify – are designed to elicit convergent thinking and group processes (Briggs & de Vreede, 2009; Briggs et al., 2009). *Convergence* increases group problem solving effectiveness because it reduces cognitive load by means of removing redundant, irrelevant, misplaced, and unclear information (Briggs & de Vreede, 2009). Specifically, the reduce pattern of collaboration entails reducing the number of concepts generated by the group to a select pool of concepts deemed worthy of further attention (Briggs et al., 2006). One sub-pattern of reduction is the *elimination/filtering* of unwanted information that does not meet certain criterion. Another sub-pattern of reduction is the *summarization* of information such that the substantive essence of a collection of information is captured in fewer words and ideas. In other words, many concepts are encapsulated within fewer and more focused concepts. Summarizations may focus on unique information, similarities across ideas, or a representative instance that capture the information (Kolfschoten & de Vreede, 2007). A third method of reduction is to reduce information through abstraction. *Abstraction* makes concepts more cognitively manageable by focusing on relevant information and disregarding the details. A sub-type of abstraction – *generalization* – occurs when a set of similar things is captured under the umbrella of a generic object. *Aggregation*, another sub-type of abstraction occurs when a relationship between two concepts is subsumed under a higher-level concept.

Clarify

The clarify pattern of collaboration increases the understanding group members share in terms of concepts, words, problems, and possible solutions (Briggs et al., 2006). The clarity pattern is best described by the two sub-patterns it is comprised of: *shared understanding* and *sense making* (Kolfschoten & de Vreede, 2007). Shared understanding refers to mutual understanding of knowledge, beliefs, and assumptions. Groups demonstrate this during collaboration when they hold a common understanding of concepts, words, and phrases. The sub-pattern *sense making* requires a certain degree of shared understanding of concepts and also includes shared understanding of the problem at-hand. Essentially, sense making prepares the group to act in a prepared and informed manner because everyone shares the same definition of the problem, as well as the same arsenal of actions for achieving the group goal. Many times, both reduce and clarify patterns are initiated by a single thinkLet, such as a FastFocus, because when comparing a reasonable number of ideas it does not take a lot of cognitive resources to identify both redundant and unclear ideas at the same time.

Organize

The organize pattern increases group understanding of the concepts of interest by ensuring that group members have mutual agreement on which relationships exist between concepts (Kolfschoten & de Vreede, 2007). Consequently, organizational patterns are particularly helpful because they reduce the effort of a follow-up activity (Briggs & de Vreede, 2009). Three sub-patterns of collaboration are subsumed under the organize pattern: *categorization*, *sequencing,* and *causal decomposition* (Kolfschoten & de Vreede, 2007). First, categorization – also known as *classification* – is the most common organizational pattern. Categorization refers to the basic cognitive task of putting information into classes or categories. Second, sequencing typically apples to workflow and refers to determining the order information is shared and tasks are conducted. Third, causal decomposition refers to the group's understanding of the causal relationships found between concepts of interest.

Evaluate

The function of the evaluate pattern is to move the group from less to more understanding of the value of concepts in regards to reaching the agreed goal (Briggs et al., 2006). The two primary purposes of an evaluation pattern are to provide support for decision making and group communication (Cheng &

Deek, 2007). One sub-pattern of evaluation – *communication of preference* – can assist in achieving both of these goals. *Reflecting* sub-patterns, which also aid in idea generation – help a group evaluate concepts by means of determining the extent to which a group collectively values each concept as a contribution toward goal achievement.

Evaluate patterns can use voting, rating, and evaluative dialogue activities to assess group preferences (Kolfschoten & de Vreede, 2007). Voting and rating are considered quantitative assessments of preferences that are collected at the individual level, but can be aggregated at the team level. These quantitative measures can identify group agreement/disagreement, preferences, and assumptions. It is useful to average all individual members' ratings into a single group rating because this analysis assigns a specific number to the perceived value of a concept. Notably, if the standard deviation of individual scores is high, this indicates that a group disagrees on the value of a concept.

There are three primary criteria for aggregating group preference voting/rating that should be considered when selecting a thinkLets evaluation activity: 1) majority rule, 2) consensus rule, and 3) selection based on expertise (Kolfschoten & de Vreede, 2007). Majority rule requires a predetermined number or percent of members to approve a concept in order for it to be considered valued by the group. Technically, if more than 50% of members agree on a judgment, that constitutes majority rule. Consensus rule requires that the group agrees on the judgment (i.e., value or preference) of a concept. Consensus is determined through an assessment of standard deviation as described in the previous paragraph. Selection based on expertise allows people with the most knowledge of the concept to make the final decision on how it is used. Frequently, experts will consider the group's rating and degree of consensus on the concept when making their final evaluation.

There are also evaluation thinkLets that can effectively support concept assessment by providing a qualitative assessment. Most of these collaboration methods require group members to share what they feel are the pros and cons of each concept. Before the decision making process reaches this stage, there should be a decent understanding of the concepts; therefore, an evaluation activity should be focused on assessing the desirability of concepts. In other words, the facilitator should not let group members argue about the wording of concepts, or get carried away with a discussion of the meaning of a concept to the point where they are splitting hairs.

One of the greatest challenges a facilitator faces during the evaluation stage of a thinkLets-based process is displaying the results of group member voting/rating in a manner that is easy to understand. In order to alleviate this headache, it is wise to find-out what deliverable product the problem owner desires.

© The Center for Collaboration Science

For example, does the problem owner desire a final list of decisions that is narrowed down to the single best solution, a list of the five best solutions, or a list of all the solutions the group rated as acceptable? Also, what level of group agreement does the problem owner require on the final solution(s)? If stringent agreement is required, the facilitator needs to identify the standard deviation of group ratings and build consensus on ratings that show poor agreement. Building consensus is discussed in the next section. Importantly, the facilitator should know ahead of time what visual depiction(s) of the results are going to be shown to the session participants. It is also important to stress that a final report of the results will be provided to the problem owner that includes a more technical analysis and a list of the concepts that did not make the final cut.

Build Consensus

Consensus refers to the extent to which group members accept or agree upon judgment of a given concept (Briggs et al., 2005). A consensus pattern of collaboration can be established by implementing the sub-patterns of *building agreement* and *building consensus* (Kolfschoten & de Vreede, 2009). Building agreement requires establishing where and why differences in preference occur. Discussion of identified differences should reveal whether these differences in preference are a result of different understandings of a concept, or true differences in opinion. Another sub-pattern of consensus building is *building commitment*. ThinkLets designed to build commitment enhance the group problem solving process by increasing the willingness of participants to commit to supporting a concept (Kolfschoten & de Vreede, 2007). Both sub-patterns can be achieved through either methods of preference aggregation, or through resolving points of disagreement. Resolving points of disagreement can be done through negotiation, increasing shared understanding of concepts, and including or excluding aspects of a concept the group disagrees on. When it seems that disagreement may have occurred due to a misunderstanding, or people may have changed their opinion of a concept, a re-vote can be used to confirm such a hypothesis. An advantage of re-voting, in comparison to making a decision based on group conversation is that anonymous voting allows participants to give their true opinion free from social pressures.

Briggs et al. (2005) identify five scenarios of group disagreement that facilitators should anticipate. In some cases, group members possess different, non-overlapping information which may lead to different perceptions of a concept. Disagreement may occur during the evaluation stage of decision making because group members disagree on the meaning of certain labels assigned to information. Different mental models of what cause and effect relationships are expected to result from or influence a concept can lead to differences in the perceived effectiveness of a concept. The two most difficult disagreements to resolve involve disagreement of goals and disagreements of taste/opinion.

The greatest challenge for the facilitator during a consensus building pattern of collaboration is to keep the discussion of concepts constructive and prevent personal attacks and heated debates from getting out of control. When discussion of a concept leads to what seems to be consensus, the group or facilitator can decide to immediately accept the decision made by the group, or a re-vote can be conducted. In this case, the facilitator has to be skilled in perceiving whether true consensus has been reached from the discussion, or there may be reason to believe that not everyone is on board with the preference of other group members. A group member admitting that he or she had voted against the majority of the group and has changed his or her mind is a good indication that a re-vote may not be necessary.

Summary

ThinkLets are designed to support the collaborative process through six primary sub-patterns of collaboration: generate, clarify, reduce, organize, evaluate, and build consensus on ideas within a group. Generally speaking, the utility of thinkLets in isolating independent stages of group problem solving is extremely valuable. For instance, if people are trying to evaluate other people's ideas (and their own) when the group is brainstorming, then they become distracted from generating high quality ideas of their own. Research consistently indicates that during a problem solving effort, premature evaluation of ideas is detrimental to the quality, originality, and number of ideas generated at by individuals. Thus, thinkLets improve collaboration by preventing other problem solving steps (e.g., reduction, clarification, evaluation) from interfering with idea generation, as well as by means of reserving idea evaluation for a separate step.

Although thinkLets strengthen the facilitated collaboration process by isolating certain problem solving steps/patterns of collaboration, they also specify what steps can be combined. For instance, the reduce, clarify, and organize patterns of collaboration can be combined there are a maneageble number of ideas in a category being addressed. However, when there are several ideas being addressed, it may be best to separate the reduce and clarify steps from the organization step because participants can make better decisions focusing on one task at a time.

In all, developing an understanding of the logical order of the aforementioned patterns of collaboration, as well as learning when patterns can be combined, is critical to developing a thorough understanding of why and when thinkLets are effective.

Chapter Six

Examples of ThinkLets

Examples of thinkLets

As previously mentioned, thinkLets are designed for ease of use. They contain five main components: template, script, tool, tool configuration, and documentation. Each is given a catchy name – a template – that is analogous to the pattern of collaboration and actual actions the group will be doing when solving a problem. The script explicitly states exactly when to give participation pre-determined verbal cues. The tool component indicates what software or hardware supports each thinkLet, and the tool configuration explains when options and restrictions participants should be confined to when using a certain thinkLet and tool together. Additionally, the documentation component of a thinkLet clarifies what is supposed to happen in response to a thinkLet, as well as any additional information needed to execute a thinkLet.

This chapter provides examples of a different thinkLet for each pattern of collaboration. These examples are taken directly from a collection of actual thinkLets (Briggs & de Vreede, 2009) and reflect some of the more specific information not presented in the previous chapters. For instance, an actual thinkLet will have instructions for: *when to use, when NOT to use, what should happen, what exactly a facilitator should do* (script), and *tips for success.*

Generate Pattern Examples

DirectedBrainstorm

CHOOSE THIS THINKLET…

… to generate creative solutions.

… when you know in advance a set of prompts that would stimulate thinking in useful directions.

DO NOT CHOOSE THIS THINKLET…

… when you want people to discuss, clarify, and elaborate on ideas as they generate. Use FreeBrainstorm instead.

… when you want people with multiple, narrow perspectives to arrive at an understanding that the problem is bigger than they originally thought it to be. Use FreeBrainstorm instead.

OVERVIEW

The team generate solutions for a problem following the FreeBrainstorming rules. However, every minute or two the moderator interrupts the group to give them a new directive prompt to stimulate their thinking.

This thinkLet is called DirectedBrainstorm because the moderator directs the attention of the group to new ways of thinking.

RESULTS

Participants produce a relatively clean collection of creative ideas that respond to the brainstorming question in the context of the directive prompts. People who use DirectedBrainstorm produce a greater number of novel, useful ideas than do people who use FreeBrainstorm. There are fewer infeasible, unclear, redundant, or off-task comments with DirectedBrainstorm. However, there is also much less discussion of the ideas, and therefore less shared understanding and less acceptance of the ideas than after a FreeBrainstorm.

DURATION

A DirectedBrainstorm typically lasts 30-40 minutes. However, for tasks with severe time constraints (e.g. generating options for emergency response) a DirectedBrainstorm may run for only 5 – 7 minutes. For complex, highly-detailed open-ended tasks like software requirements negotiation, a DirectedBrainstorm may last as long as 90-120 minutes at a sitting.

PREPARATION

Required Information

You will need the following information to complete this thinkLet successfully:

- A Brainstorming Question

- A collection of directive prompts – statements to stimulate participants to think about the question in new ways. You can cycle through your prompts several times, and you can change their wording as you go to keep things interesting. Directive prompts usually pertain to the criteria for judging the quality of an idea. For example:

  - *"Give me ideas that would be fast to implement..."*

  - *"Think of ideas that would be acceptable to these stakeholders..."*

  - *"Give me ideas that would be inexpensive to implement..."*

Sometimes you might choose <u>comparative</u> prompts that ask participants to come up with solutions that better along some dimension than the ideas that were already submitted. Such prompts might look something like this:

- *"Give me a solution that is more likely to reduce production time than would the ideas you see in front of you."*

- *"Now give me a solution that is more likely to produce higher quality products than would any of the ideas you see in front of you."*

- *"Now contribute a solution that would be more likely to improve consistency of quality than would any of the previous ideas you see in front of you."*

- *"Think of a solution that would be more likely to cut production costs than any of ideas you've seen so far."*

If you were working with a team to improve conditions at an overcrowded university, you might prepare a list of Directed prompts before the meeting that looked like this:

- *"Give me ideas that make it more likely to...*

  - *...cut class size."*

  - *...reduce faculty workload."*

  - *...bring in immediate cash."*

  - *...improve graduation rates."*

Required Capabilities

For a DirectedBrainstorm, your team should have tools that allow them to do the following:

- A page for each participant and one extra page per each 10 participants.

- Only one participant at-a-time can view and add brainstorming contributions to each page.

- Participants must be able to swap to a different page after each contribution.

- One separate page for the moderator to record directive prompts.

- Moderator may view, add, edit, re-order, and delete directive prompts.

Here is a way to implement DirectedBrainstorm on paper and in GroupSystems:

DirectedBrainstorm on Paper	DirectedBrainstorm in GroupSystems
• Provide each participant with a sheet of paper. • Provide the moderator with an extra sheet of paper for each 10 participants in the group. • Provide the moderator with a separate sheet of paper to record the brainstorming prompts.	• In the Electronic Brainstorming module, add as many discussion sheets as there are participants. • Add an extra discussion sheet for each 10 participants in the group. • Enter the brainstorming question. • Set the brainstorming question to display as the heading for participant pages.

EXECUTION RULES

To run a successful DirectedBrainstorm, the following rules have to be followed:

• Participants may view only one page at a time.

• Participants contribute only one idea to a page they are viewing.

• Contributions should be made anonymously.

• A participant must swap to a new page after each contribution.

• Participants may respond to contributions of others in one of three ways:

  • Ignore existing ideas and add a new idea.

  • Elaborate or build upon an idea.

- Criticize or argue against an idea.

SAMPLE SCRIPT

The following sample script will help you execute the above rules and run an effective DirectedBrainstorm:

Do This

1. Develop a set of directive prompts based the goals the group seeks to attain. (For instructions and examples see the *Required Information* section above.)

2. Explain and clarify the brainstorming question.

3. Explain and clarify the structure and nature of useful responses to the brainstorming question.

4. Draw participant attention to the pages upon which their brainstorming will begin.

Say This

5. Invite the participants to start:

   a. On Paper: *"Please take a pen and a piece of brainstorming paper."*

   b. In GroupSystems: *"Please click the 'Go' button to open a brainstorming page."*

6. *"Each of you is starting on a different page."*

7. Provide the first prompt to the participants: *"Please contribute the single best idea in response to our brainstorming question that you can think of. In particular, think of ideas that are <directive criterion>."*

8. *"When you have contributed your idea...*

   a. On Paper: *hold up your brainstorming page and I will come to you and hand you another brainstorming page."*

   b. In GroupSystems: *click the "Submit" button to send your contribution to the group. When you click submit, the system will take away the page you are working on, and will automatically jump you to a different page."*

9. *"The new page may contain ideas contributed by other participants."*

10. *"When you see the contributions of others, you may respond in one of three ways"*

    a. *You may argue against it."*

    b. *You may elaborate or build upon it."*

    c. *You may be inspired to a completely new idea."*

11. *"Our goal is to get as many different ideas as we can in a short amount of time."*

12. *"Any questions? You may begin."*

Do This   13. At pre-determined intervals (say, 2-to-4 minutes) interrupt the group by announcing a new directive prompt.

Say This   14. *"Please keep contributing your ideas in response to our brainstorming question. In particular, now think of ideas that are <new directive criterion>."*

Do This   15. Repeat the pattern of swapping pages and responding to directed prompts until the group runs out of time or ideas. If you run out of prompts before the group runs out of ideas, you may repeat the prompts.

INSIGHTS

Essence (How it works)

DirectedBrainstorm is a variation of the FreeBrainstorm thinkLet. The essence of the FreeBrainstorm lies in three elements: a) having the participants swap to a new page after each contribution; b) allowing participants to make anonymous contributions, and c) allowing participants to criticize the ideas of others. Directed brainstorming adds one more essential element to the activity. The facilitator interrupts the group periodically to provide a directive prompt that stimulates the participants to think about the problem in a new way. Directive prompts typically relate to criteria for judging the quality of the ideas generated. However, other kinds of prompts may also be used to good effect.

Effects

Participants in a DirectedBrainstorm tend to produce about twice as many high-quality ideas as those in a FreeBrainstorm, with fewer irrelevant contributions. Consequently, it is often faster to reduce and clarify the idea set in a follow-on step. Unlike the FreeBrainstorm, however, the participants do little criticizing, discussing, and elaborating on the ideas of others. Therefore, they do not tend to develop the broad understanding of the problem space which the FreeBrainstorming produces. They also feel less buy-in to their ideas when they are done.

Why it works

The mechanisms of the brain that give rise to creative ideas thrive on the variety of stimuli they receive. In FreeBrainstorming, the contributions of others serve as stimuli. In DirectedBrainstorm, you have the additional stimuli of the directive prompts. Each Directive prompt triggers a new train of thought, bringing a new set of concepts into the creative mix.

Pitfalls

Less Buy-in. After a DirectedBrainstorm, participants feel less certainty about the merits of the ideas they generated than do participants in a FreeBrainstorm. They also feel less certain that others understand the ideas they contributed. It is therefore useful to follow a DirectedBrainstorm with an activity that allows for oral discussion of the ideas, like a FastFocus ThinkLet.

Fast and high quality, but not necessarily exhaustive. The DirectedBrainstorm thinkLet is very fast and very focused. You tend to get good quality solutions, and the quality tends to get better as the process unfolds. There is very little noise in the results. People don't contribute silly and bad ideas, and they don't make comments about other people's ideas. This means that it takes far less time to converge on the key issues when the brainstorming is over.

However, this lack of noise can be a two-edged sword. In FreeBrainstorming people tend to argue with and elaborate on ideas. In DirectedBrainstorm they do not. Silly and bad ideas can be useful for pushing people outside the box, to explore the boundaries of their problem space and their solution space. Further, un-discussed and unchallenged ideas may be less well-understood and less useful than ideas that have been kicked around. So make sure you schedule a discussion to follow a DirectedBrainstorm.

The Duet Danger. Eric Santanen, a creativity researcher, made an intriguing discovery: the order in which you present the directive prompts has a significant impact on the number of creative ideas the group will generate. Eric conducted an experiment where 61 groups worked to generate solutions for humanitarian relief for a flood-ravaged third-world town whose water supply had been contaminated. He had five criteria for idea quality:

© The Center for Collaboration Science

- Provided sufficient water.

- Fast.

- Inexpensive.

- Easy to implement.

- Required minimal heavy equipment.

He derived 4 directive prompts for each criterion, for a total of 20 prompts. He had people brainstorm for 40 minutes. Every two minutes he gave them a directive prompt. For one third of the groups, he organized the prompts so that he presented all four prompts for one criterion, then all four prompts for the next criterion, then all four for the next, and so on. He called that the Quartet treatment because the groups received four prompts on the same topic before they switched to a new topic. For one third of the groups, he organized the same 20 prompts into a different order, so that he presented two prompts on one topic, then two prompts on the next topic, then two on the next, and so on. He called that the Duet treatment because the groups responded to two prompts on a topic before switching topics. For one third of the groups he presented one prompt for each topic, then another prompt for each topic, and so on. Thus, the groups switched topics with every new prompt. He called this the Solo treatment.

The results were rather startling. People who used the Quartet arrangement and people who used the Solo arrangement produced more than twice as many creative ideas as those who used the Duet treatment. It took a while to figure out why that happened. Here's the answer. There is creative benefit from thinking about a new topic, but there is cognitive cost for switching topics. There is also creative benefit from following a train of thought for a while. So the Solo groups got the benefit of many changes of topic. The Quartet groups got the benefit of following a train of thought for a while. The Duet groups, however, didn't get the benefit of many new topics, and didn't get the benefit of following one train of thought for a while. As a result, they were less productive. So the lesson is, either switch topics with every prompt, or let them pursue the same topic for several prompts, but don't lead them in a Duet.

SUCCESS STORY

We once worked with a team of eight planners on the command ship for the U.S. Navy's Third Fleet. During field maneuvers, it was this team's job was to listen to intelligence briefings, and then to try to guess what the enemy might be doing. They would hold an oral discussion, then brief their commander on the enemy's most likely, least likely, and most dangerous courses of action, given the available intelligence. This process took about 90 minutes, during which the team typically considered four to six possibilities.

The team agreed to try a Directed brainstorming approach with the following prompts:

- *"What is the enemy's most likely course of action? Now swap pages."*

- *"Now tell something they might do that would be far more surprising than the idea you see before you. Now swap pages again."*

- *"Now think of something they might do that would be far more dangerous than either of the ideas on the screen in front of you. Swap pages again."*

The team completed eight cycles in seven minutes, producing 56 possible courses of action the enemy might be preparing to take.

The team followed up with a BucketShuffle thinkLet, and in under half-an-hour was prepared to brief the commander on the most likely, least likely, and most dangerous courses of action the enemy might be pursuing, having engaged in a discussion with far more breadth and depth than had been possible using conventional means.

Convergence (Reduce and Clarify) Pattern Examples

BucketWalk

(Reduce & Clarify)
CHOOSE THIS THINKLET…

… To reduce the number of ideas in one or more categories of ideas by eliminating redundant or irrelevant ideas, and to establish shared understanding of the ideas that remain.

… To validate that ideas have been correctly placed in the categories to which they have been assigned, for example, following a Popcorn Sort, LeafHopper, or other organizing thinkLet or a OnePage generating thinkLet.

DO NOT CHOOSE THIS THINKLET…

… if there are so many ideas to address that the group would become restless and tired during the process, and so lose focus. Consider a BucketBriefing thinkLet instead.

OVERVIEW

In BucketWalk, you verify an earlier organization process. After a PopcornSort team members review the contents of each bucket to make sure that all items are appropriately placed and understood. Moreover, cases of overlap between items are resolved.

BucketWalk is so named because the participants "walk" through the contents of each category at a leisurely pace, contemplating whether anything in a given category actual fits better in a different category or should be phrased more appropriately. The word, *bucket*, is often used in ThinkLet names as a metaphor for *category*.

RESULTS

The BucketWalk produces lists of unique ideas (no duplicates) within one or more categories that are clearly expressed, whose meanings are agreed by the group, that are expressed at a useful level of abstraction, and that are relevant to the categories in which they are placed.

DURATION

The time required for a BucketWalk will vary widely depending on the number of categories, the number of ideas in the categories, the degree to which the ideas have already been refined and explained in earlier steps, and the degree to of consensus that exists from the outset about which ideas belong to which categories. For a BucketWalk through five, each with about 15 ideas, most of which are already clear to the group, and most of which are already well-placed, we would typically plan about 30 minutes. But we have seen BucketWalks take as few as 10 minutes and as long as 4 hours, depending on the task.

You can shorten a BucketWalk by eliminating screening criteria, for example, by ignoring redundancies and clarifications and focusing only on whether ideas belong in the category where they have been placed.

PREPARATION

Required Information

The following information needs to be available to execute a BucketWalk:

- A set of ideas in one or more categories.

Required Capabilities

For this thinkLet, you need to have the following capabilities available:

- A page for each category, viewable by all team members

- The ability to draw the team members' attention to the category under review

- The ability for a moderator to add, edit, and delete ideas within a category

- The ability for a moderator to move ideas among category

This is how you can implement these capabilities on paper and in GroupSystems:

BucketWalk on Paper	BucketWalk in GroupSystems
• Designate a space on the wall, or perhaps a flip-chart page for each category • Display a label for each category • Cut apart ideas so each is on its own slip of paper. • Write a unique number next to each idea so the group can discuss them by number (e.g. "Idea 3 and Idea 17 are really express the same concept with different words."). • Tape all the ideas for a given category in its designated	• GroupSystems Categorizer Tool. • Participants can only see ideas. • Participant cannot add, move, or copy ideas.

EXECUTION RULES

In order to execute a successful BucketWalk, the following rules have to be followed:

- Discuss the ideas in a single category at a time.

- Finish discussing all issues in a single category before moving on to the next.

- The discussion should only focus on the content of the ideas in a category in order to determine whether they are clearly formulated, placed in the right category, or possibly overlapping with other ideas. Participants should not discuss the merits of the ideas.

SAMPLE SCRIPT

The following script allows you run an effective BucketWalk following the above rules:

Do This	1. Draw the team's attention to the first category:
	a. <u>On Paper</u>: Direct the team's attention with gestures and words
	b. <u>In GroupSystems</u>: Double-click the bucket for the first category. The ideas in that category will appear. Use the Match-Views feature to open the same bucket on participant screens.
Say This	2. "Is there anything in this bucket which does not belong here? Are any

of the ideas duplicates of other ideas? Are there any ideas you don't understand? If so, please tell me the numbers and we will discuss it."

Do this   3. If any participant raises an issue with one or more ideas in the set:

      a. Allow the participant to explain the issue

      b. Moderate and oral discussion of the issue, and propose a solution to the group (e.g. "Shall I re-write the idea to read like this <proposed new wording>? Shall I move this to this other category? Shall we use the wording in Number 3 and eliminate Number 17 because it is redundant?").

      c. When the group acquiesces to your proposal, execute it.

      4. Repeat Steps 2 and 3 until nobody proposes additional revisions to the ideas in the category.

Do This   5. If there are more categories to address, then draw the team's attention to the next category.

      6. Repeat Steps 2 – 5

INSIGHTS

Essence (How it works)

The essence of the BucketWalk is in the systematic examination of one category at a time for three kinds of issues: a) items that do not belong in the category; b) items that group members do not understand (perhaps because they are poorly worded, or because they use jargon with which some team members are unfamiliar); and c) duplicate items.

Effects

Usually the team will find two or three items in each category that might belong in a different category. If the team concurs, you move such items into another bucket. Sometimes they

      © The Center for Collaboration Science

will find an item for which no category yet exists. Then, the group must either decide that the idea is not relevant to their work, or they must create a new category. Often, participants point out problems with comprehension of items because they are poorly phrased. You resolve these through some verbal discussion asking for alternatives, and suggesting alternative wordings yourself. If the participants discover redundant ideas, you ask the team which wording is best, and which idea(s) should be removed in favor of the best wording. The group may want you to edit the idea to combine the best of several phrases into a single expression of the idea.

By the end of the BucketWalk, your team will have confidence that the items in each category belong in that category, that the categories are cleaned up, and that the categories themselves make sense. They will also have a better shared understanding of what each category means, what each contains, and what the contents mean.

Why it works

Cognitive load is less when participants consider only one category at a time instead of the whole collection of ideas. Typically participants will call for the moving of 2 or 3 ideas out of a category, and will clarify the meanings of 2 or 3 others.

A BucketWalk often follows a PopcornSort. Where the Popcorn Sort feels fast and wild and fun, the BucketWalk feels leisurely and contemplative.

People often don't believe that their ideas have been understood by others until they've had a chance to discuss them aloud. This thinkLet provides an oral discussion at a time when the group is typically trying to create shared meaning.

Pitfalls

Bucket Wars. Progress may stall when team members begin to debate the category into which an idea best fits. Unless it is critical to have each idea in exactly one category, this kind of debate can be quickly defused by offering to copy the idea into both categories.

Merit Debates. Sometimes a participant may start a debate about whether an idea is a good or a bad idea, which can stall the BucketWalk. If it appears that the debate will go beyond a one or two sentence exchange, you can cut it off by saying, "Right now we are not debating the merits of these ideas. We are only checking to see whether they are in the right category, whether they are well understood, and whether they are redundant. We will be evaluating the ideas in a few minutes. Please hold your evaluative comments until then.

SUCCESS STORY

A customer support organization within a commercial company brainstormed its goals, and then PopcornSorted them into 7 categories. When they BucketWalked the categories, they found that two of the categories had strong overlap. They merged those two categories. They shifted about a dozen goals from one category to another, and create one new category when they discovered one set of words had been used to describe two very different kinds of goals. The resulting validated, organized goal sets became the foundation for developing a new reward system for the personnel in the customer support organization.

BroomWagon

(reduce pattern)

CHOOSE THIS THINKLET…

… if your team has generated a large number of items (50 – 300) and they need to reduce them to quickly focus on the key items only.

… when it is not necessary or desirable that the team analyses each item in detail.

… when choices are largely a matter of preference.

© The Center for Collaboration Science

DO NOT CHOOSE THIS THINKLET…

… when you need to arrive at a final list in which each item is evaluated carefully. For this, you need to use an Evaluate thinkLet. BroomWagon just provides a first pass to help a group reduce the number of issues that they need to consider in future steps.

… when you need the team to make a decision, e.g. to pick the three most important courses of action. BroomWagon is not suited for decision making, only for filtering ideas down to a most-popular sub-set.

… when an analysis based on rational criteria should supersede a selection based on preference.

OVERVIEW

In this thinkLet, the team quickly filters a set of ideas to zero in on the ones worthy of further attention. When you deal with a team facing many issues, items, or ideas, use BroomWagon to sieve out the items on which the team needs to focus. BroomWagon allows you to let the team reduce an unmanageable number of items to a manageable number. BroomWagon could be used to winnow some of the chaff from the wheat before trying to polish or make sense of the items contributed during a brainstorming activity.

This thinkLet is called BroomWagon because it works the same way as a BroomWagon in cycle courses. For example, in the "Tour de France", a truck – the BroomWagon – will pick up cyclists that fall behind and won't make the finish line in time. In other words, the cyclists that won't make the cut, and swept up. The BroomWagon thinkLet sweeps ideas off the table that the team will not consider any further.

RESULTS

A selection of items from a large set that the team agrees are worth more attention.

DURATION

Using BroomWagon it normally takes about 15 minutes to come down from 200 ideas to about 15 to 20. The time required varies proportionately with the number of starting ideas and the number you want to end up with.

PREPARATION

Required Information

For this thinkLet, you need to have the following information in place to successfully execute it:

- The set of ideas that the team will select from, for example the results from a FreeBrainstorm or a ComparativeBrainstorm activity.

- Each idea in the set should be unique. Since team members will select the ideas they like most, there should be no overlap among these ideas.

- An end target in terms of the number of ideas that the team can continue working on. This target number does not have to be exact; often it represents a range, for example 10-15 ideas.

Required Capabilities

For this thinkLet, you need to provide your team with the following:

- Everyone must be able to see all ideas that are being considered.

- Everyone must have the ability to select between 20% and 33% of these ideas. For example, if the main lists consists of 47 ideas, each team member may select up to 15 ideas.

Here is how you can implement BroomWagon on paper and in GroupSystems:

BroomWagon on Paper	**BroomWagon in GroupSystems**
• Hang all ideas individually on a wall. • Give each team member a number of voting stickers, between 20% and 33% of the total number of ideas.	• Put a list of all ideas in the Vote module. • Select the Multiple Selection voting method in the Vote module and allow team members to select between 20 and 33 percent of the total number of ideas.
	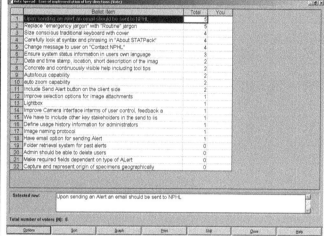

EXECUTION RULES

The key rules that you have to maintain for the BroomWagon to be effective include:

- Each team member gets to select between 20% and 33% of the ideas under consideration.

- Ideas that receive no or few votes are removed from further consideration.

- Focus on removing groups of ideas, rather than individual ideas one by one.

SAMPLE SCRIPT

The following script will help you to execute the above rules and run an effective BroomWagon:

Say this:	1.	*"We have a set of brainstorming ideas here that we will need to filter before we continue. We do not have enough resources to continue working on every idea during the remainder of meeting. Therefore, I want you to read through the ideas and check the ones that you think merit more attention."*
	2.	*"I will now give you a number checkmarks, so you can only check so many ideas."*
Do this:	3(a)	On paper: Give each team member their voting stickers.
	3(b)	In GroupSystems: Start the team members in the Vote module.
Say this:	4.	*"Please go ahead, and place your checkmarks."*
Do this:	5.	Wait for each team member to place his or her checkmarks.
Say this:	6.	*"Let's have a look at the results. There are a number of items that got few or no votes. Let's remove these from further consideration as they appear to be less important than the other ones."*
	7.	*"Now let's look at the ones that received a couple of votes. We do not have*

enough time to address all ideas, so I propose that we do not further consider these ideas either."

Consider this:

8. As long as the team agrees, continue removing groups of ideas from the bottom up (i.e. with fewest votes) until you end up with the maximum number of ideas that you want to handle from that moment onward.

9. If the team argues that they do not want to have more ideas removed, yet you still have too many to continue working with, then let them mark their critical preferences again. Of course, you will have to squeeze the number of checkmarks to 20%-33% of the remaining number of ideas. Say this:

  a. *"Let's vote again. I will give you new checkmarks. Please check the items that you feel merit further attention."*

Normally, you will achieve your desired end target number of ideas in at most 3 iterations, depending on the length of the original list.

INSIGHTS

Essence (How it works)

BroomWagon is an effective way to trim down a long list of items to a short list. Teams like the process because it easy to understand and carry out. The essential part of this thinkLet is that you have to focus the team on the 'loosing' ideas rather than the 'winning' ideas. After a voting activity, you normally draw the team's attention to the top ranked ideas. Yet with BroomWagon you focus them on the lowest ranked ideas. The reason is that few, if any, team members can and will argue that the lowest ranked ideas need to be kept. So, these can be removed with little pain. Working your way up through the results, you filter the least important ideas out.

Effects

With BroomWagon you will let the team separate key issues from less important issues. The team will filter down to a most-popular subset so that they can be persuaded to focus their attention on the ideas that are considered more critical. Be aware that some useful ideas may be swept away as BroomWagon does not produce an exhaustive set of useful ideas.

BroomWagon will *not* help you to sort a list into categories of importance (for example 'high', 'medium', 'low'), nor will it let you walk away with a finely tuned order of ideas. If you need to organize a list of ideas in terms of merit categories, consider doing a ClusterVote. If you need to establish priorities between ideas, consider a StrawRate or MultiCriteria.

Often the BroomWagon process proceeds very fast in the beginning. Then, towards the end, the pace appears to be slowing down. This is because it is easier for people to make the first selections than to place the last few checkmarks. To keep the pace going, you may jokingly stimulate the slower participants saying: *"Remember that the last person to express their preference will have to pay for the refreshments during the next break!"*

Why it works (Possibly not included?)

The key to the BroomWagon's success lies in its low cognitive load for the team members and the number of checkmarks used.

Low cognitive load. BroomWagon is a great way to have teams go through long lists of ideas. Teams do not have to consider each idea in detail. They only have to tick the few ideas they like. Imagine having to evaluate 50 ideas on a 7 point scale versus just ticking off the 15 ideas you think are most critical and want to consider in more detail. The latter activity requires much less cognitive effort and increases the pace of the workshop.

Number of checkmarks. A key characteristic of BroomWagon is the number of checkmarks that you give the team. You should give them enough marks for the good stuff. But you do not want to give them too many as then every item will likely receive at least one vote. This will make it more difficult to remove items off the list. We found that different facilitators have different rules of thumb for deciding how many checkmarks to give each person. The lowest we've seen is 20% of the items. The highest we've seen is 33%. Just pick a number in this range that seems to suit you and the situation.

Pitfalls

Although the BroomWagon represents a straightforward way to filter key ideas from a larger set, there are a number of pitfalls that you have to be aware of. Each of these are easy to recognize and mitigate.

Redundant ideas. Remember that if you perform a BroomWagon on raw brainstorming ideas, there are undoubtedly redundancies and ambiguities in the list. So, if a certain idea is appearing half-a-dozen times in various forms in the list, people may spread their votes across those items. This is a problem. A critical idea that appears more than once in theory list, may be swept off because each of its manifestations does make the 'cut'. To deal with this, you may consider the Concentration thinkLet before the BroomWagon to remove redundancy.

Lack of clarity on ideas. Sometimes people protest at the start of the BroomWagon. *"We can't vote on this list; the ideas are not clear."* It may be they did not have enough time to familiarize themselves with the ideas on the list. It may also be that they want to influence the outcome of the BroomWagon by presenting their preferences during an oral discussion. In these situations, you may quickly walk-through the list asking people to identify items that are not clear and have someone explain them. Alternatively, you may perform TheLobbyist thinkLet just before inviting the team to vote.

Indecisiveness. Some people have difficulty focusing and distinguishing between really important items and less important items. They say for example, *"I need more checkmarks; there are just too many ideas that are important."* The way to handle this situation is by stressing that the team only has limited resources available to do deal with every ideas. Then you may offer this person a more methodical approach: *"Why don't you start with the single most important item on the list. Mark this. Then mark the single most important item of what remains. Please place your checkmarks in this order."*

Evenly spread preferences. In theory, it may happen that every idea on the list receives a similar number of votes. In this case, you have no basis to decide which ideas you can remove. The problem may be that people all voted for their own pet ideas. You can address this by handing out fewer checkmarks so that they have to select even among their own pet ideas.

Resistance to removal. At various times, people find it difficult to accept their pet idea being swept from the list. They start protesting: *"You can't remove *that* idea, it's the best on the list."* If the team agreed in advance to remove all ideas that receive fewer that a certain number of votes, you may remind everyone of that agreement. If you have a next round of voting ahead of you, you can also suggest that the ideas remains on the list provided that it be removed without discussion in the next round if it does not meet the cut. Alternatively, you may execute the Lobbyist thinkLet to give every participant equal opportunity to promote their pet idea and then vote again.

Strategic behavior in manual groups. When you execute the BroomWagon on paper, per the guidelines described above, you may at times run into two types of strategic behavior. Some people may want to place multiple checkmarks on a single idea so that they increase the chances of the idea making it to the next round. Some people may wait until everyone else is done placing their voting stickers, so that they can see which ideas need no further support and they can boost other ideas. You can ask people to place not more than one voting sticker per idea, and you can ask people to not linger around, but if someone is bend upon this type of behavior you cannot prevent it. If you want to rule out this behavior, you need to implement the paper BroomWagon differently: Make sure every idea has a unique identification number. Then, give every team member a piece of paper and ask them to write down the identification numbers of the ideas they feel are critical to keep. Instruct them not to write down more than a certain number of ideas (between 20%-35% of the total number). Finally, you collect the papers and then tally the votes on a flipover or in a spreadsheet.

The bottom line is that during a BroomWagon exercise, some painful moments may occur. People may protest against getting rid of some ideas, people may challenge the number of checkmarks they get, etc. It is therefore important to consider process rules before charging the team with a BroomWagon. We suggest such process rules as:

- *"The group consists of 9 people. Let's say that each idea that receives 3 votes or less is dropped from the list."*

- *"We have 258 ideas here. In the remainder of our workshop, we will deal with about a dozen at most. So let's iterate until we have identified about a dozen key issues."*

SUCCESS STORY

BroomWagon has been used hundreds of times with groups all around the world. It's easy and effective. It turned out to be a big success in a workshop in the Port of Rotterdam, the Netherlands, the largest harbor in the world. Here a conglomerate of harbor parties was discussing future e-commerce initiatives. The team generated about 75 project ideas in 25 minutes. They wanted to elaborate on about 10 project ideas in terms of a project plan description. The BroomWagon procedure was used for 15 minutes including two iterations. They ended up with 9 project ideas that were subsequently worked out in more detail.

Organize Pattern Example

ChauffeurSort

(Organize)

CHOOSE THIS THINKLET...

… if your team must organize a set of ideas into a set of categories, and it is important that they carefully consider the appropriate category for each idea.

… if creating shared understanding of the categories is as important as the actual placement of the ideas in the categories.

DO NOT CHOOSE THIS THINKLET...

… if a team needs to organize a set of ideas quickly. A PopcornSort followed by BucketWalk is usually far faster.

… if it is not important to assure that each idea gets into precisely the correct category the first time. Consider the PopcornSort thinkLet instead, which is much faster.

… consider following the PopcornSort with a BucketWalk if participants wish to validate the contents of each category after the PopcornSort.

OVERVIEW

With this thinkLet, you guide a team in organizing a set of ideas into a number of categories. Team members discuss the fit of each idea in one or more pre-defined categories before it is placed. Categories may have been defined before the workshop, or they may be derived during the workshop with thinkLets like ThemeSeeker or RichRelations.

This thinkLet derives its name from the role of the facilitator in this process. The team give directions on where to place each idea, while the facilitator ensures that each ideas arrives at its designated destination.

RESULTS

A set of ideas organized into categories. The team members agree with the placement.

DURATION

The time required to execute a ChauffeurSort depends on the number of ideas that need to be organized and the level of understanding the team has about the categories. If the team has a solid understanding of the available categories, they can organize about 30 to 45 ideas per hour.

PREPARATION

Required Information

You need to have the following information in place to successfully execute a ChauffeurSort:

- The ideas that the team has to organize, for example the results from a FreeBrainstorm or a ComparativeBrainstorm activity. It is not necessary that each idea is unique.

- The categories that the ideas will be organized into.

Required Capabilities

To execute the ChauffeurSort you need to provide the team with the following:

- Each team member must be able to see each idea that has to be organized.

- Each team member must be able to see all categories.

- At any point during the process, each team member must be able to see which ideas have been placed in the various categories.

Here is how you can implement the ChauffeurSort on paper and in GroupSystems:

ChauffeurSort on Paper	ChauffeurSort in GroupSystems
• Hang labels with category names on a wall. • Have each idea available on a separate piece of paper that can be hung underneath a category label.	• List the category names as buckets in the Categorizer module. • List the ideas to be organized in the top bucket. • Let team members view ideas in buckets; do not allow them to move or copy ideas.

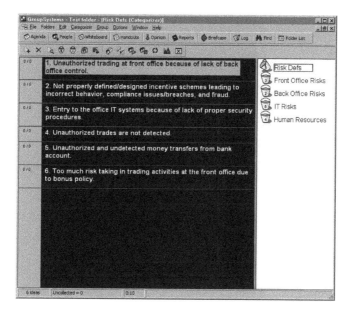

EXECUTION RULES

You have to maintain the following key rules to successfully execute the ChauffeurSort:

• Each idea is considered in turn in terms of its fit into one or more categories.

• The placement of a particular idea is completed before the next idea is considered.

• The discussion of idea placement should only focus on 'fit'. It should not focus on idea quality.

SAMPLE SCRIPT

The following script will help you to maintain the above rules and run an effective ChauffeurSort:

Say this:	3.	*"We have a set of ideas here that we need to organize into the categories that you can see here. We will consider each idea in turn. For each idea, I will ask for your suggestions about the category where it should be placed. Before we start, I will first explain the different categories."*
Do this:	4.	Introduce and explain the categories to the team.
Say this:	5.	For each idea that has to be organized, ask the team, *"In which category does this idea belong, and why?"*
Do this:	6.	Facilitate a verbal discussion about the reasons for placing the comment into a bucket.
	7.	If a team member raises issues about the quality of the idea, say this: *"At this point we are only discussing whether this ideas fits into one of these categories. The merits of the idea will be addressed in a future activity."*
	8.	If a team member raises issues about the clarity of the idea formulation, propose an improved formulation or ask the team for suggestions.
	9.	If the team cannot decide where to place the idea, put it to the side for the moment and come back to it after the other ideas have been placed.
	10.	When there is sufficient consensus about the placement of the idea:

   a. On paper: Stick the idea underneath the appropriate category label.

   b. In GroupSystems: Drag and drop the idea in the appropriate category bucket.

11. Repeat steps 3-8 until all ideas have been placed in the appropriate categories.

INSIGHTS

Essence (How it works)

The ChauffeurSort is a straightforward thinkLet to help your team organize their ideas into a known set of categories. The essence of this thinkLet is that each idea is considered in turn to agree on its placement. Because of this, the process takes much longer than a PopcornSort. However, you end up with an organized set of ideas where every idea should be in the right place so you do not have to BucketWalk the categories to check for misplacements.

Effects

During the ChauffeurSort, the team will discuss the placement of each idea in turn and reach agreement before assigning it to a particular category. As a result, the team starts building shared understanding about the nature of both the ideas and the categories. After a ChauffeurSort, a team is ready to continue working on the ideas with a better grasp of their nature and place in the larger structure of information that they are considering.

By the time the task is completed the team will have developed a good understanding of what each category does and does not mean. Yet that understanding may shift and deepen as the task continues, so it may be worth doing a final BucketWalk at the end to verify that the items placed early in the process wound up in the right categories.

Why it works

In a chauffeured sort the magic is in the discussion of the placement of every item. By asking team members to verbalize reasons for idea placement, they have to share their understanding of the ideas. This leads to an increase of shared understanding in the team which will facilitate follow-on activities. Also, by considering each idea in turn, every team member has an opportunity to see to it that his or her ideas end up in the correct categories.

Pitfalls

The key pitfall regarding the ChauffeurSort is the time it takes to complete. It is not the fastest way to organize the results from a brainstorming session. Normally, a PopcornSort followed by a BucketWalk will be far faster. However, with that combination of thinkLets the team only discusses ideas are believed to be misplaced or overlapping. Therefore, it is less likely to further shared understanding.

If you feel that it is important that the team builds some shared understanding on the categories used but you do not have the time to perform a complete ChauffeurSort, then consider doing the ChauffeurSort for the first, say, 25 percent of the ideas, and then organize the remaining ideas with the PopcornSort.

SUCCESS STORY

The Amsterdam Police Force in the Netherlands was reorganizing its Criminal Investigations Department because they were moving from a functional bureaucracy to a project-based approach were people from many specialties joined a team for a particular criminal investigation.

The reorganization team used FreeBrainstorming to develop a comprehensive set of information gathering problems they had experienced in their careers. They used an ExpertChoice thinkLet to develop a set of categories representing all the different kinds of organized crime they encountered – computer crime, drugs, racketeering, and so on. The team then did a ChauffeurSort to decide which information problems were associated with which kinds of crime. The team often put the same item in several categories. Items that applied to all categories they placed in a "General Problems" category.

The results served several purposes. Based on the contents of each category, they were able to decide what kinds of specialists should be assigned to teams investigating each kind of crime. They results also became the basis for a checklist to make sure an investigation team gathered all types of information required to build a case.

Evaluate Pattern Examples

StrawPoll

When to use:

- To determine the level of consensus in a group
- To determine points of agreement or conflict
- To evaluate a number of concepts

When NOT to use:

- To make a decision

Image from: http://voice123team.blogspot.com/

Overview:

- This thinkLet is used to assess the preferences and level of agreement held by the group. It is intended to spur discussion, as opposed to make an immediate decision.

What to do:

- Tell participants they we are going to take a StrawPoll

- Reassure them that we are not making a final decision right now, we are just trying to get a sense of the group so we can focus on where subsequent efforts should be focused

- Explain the scale they will be using to rate the items. Explicitly state what the rating numbers mean

- Tell them to submit their ballot when they are done voting, and that the votes can be changed before the final submission

Tips:

- Many different criteria can be used to evaluate items such as 10-point scale, true/false, yes/no, or agree/disagree choices

- This technique has the advantages of being fast and its anonymity allows participants to give their opinion free from social pressures

BucketWalk

Can be used to evaluate, as well as to reduce and clarify information.

See the "Convergence – Reduce and clarify section" section for details.

Image from: http://www.diytrade.com 1

Build Consensus Pattern Example

CrowBar

(Build Commitment)

CHOOSE THIS THINKLET...

… to build consensus around one or more proposals by surfacing and examining assumptions.

… to share unshared information.

… to reveal hidden agendas.

… to provoke a focused discussion about issues where the group has a low consensus.

DO NOT CHOOSE THIS THINKLET...

… if you just want the group to reduce the number of ideas in a set, without delving into the reasons behind the reduction. Consider the BroomWagon or FastFocus thinkLet instead.

OVERVIEW

This thinkLet focuses participants on the underlying reasons behind a lack of consensus. In it, people focus on one ballot item at a time, starting with the one with the highest standard of deviation. Participants are asked to speculate about what reasons might exist for differences of opinion that manifest in a polling activity (e.g. the StrawPoll thinkLet). They discuss the possible reasons proposed by their peers.

We call this thinkLet the Crowbar because it is so useful for prying assumptions and information out of a group. Sometimes this thinkLet has been the only way we could find to get people talking about the real issues.

RESULTS

This thinkLet yields an understanding of the differences in meanings, assumptions, information, goals, and tastes among participants that manifest during a polling activity.

DURATION

The duration of this activity varies widely by the number of ballot items, by the diversity of opinions within the group about each ballot item, and by the variety and sensitivity of the reasons behind those opinions. We typically plan about 3-5 minutes per ballot item, although we occasionally see a discussion of 15 minutes on a single item. If it runs much longer than that, we typically suggest that the group add it to the agenda as an item for separate discussion.

We typically don't decide how long a Crowbar thinkLet will run by guessing in advance how many ballot items there will be. Rather, we decide how much time we can afford to devote to the crowbar, and start with the item with the highest disagreement and work our way down the list as time permits. When time runs out, we still have some assurance that we have focused on the items with the most disagreement.

PREPARATION

Required Information

For the CrowBar you need to have the following information to successfully execute it:

- Ballot items from an earlier vote.
- A standard deviation or other measure of agreement for each ballot item.
- The voting criteria from the earlier vote.

Required Capabilities

To do a CrowBar you should provide your team with tools that allow them to do the following:

- A page to display polling results by ballot item viewable for all participants.
- Some measure of agreement on each ballot item (e.g. Standard Deviation) viewable for all participants.

You can implement the CrowBar thinkLet on paper and in GroupSystems as follows:

CrowBar on Paper

- Collect paper ballots from the participants.

- Set up a table in a spreadsheet to record each participant's vote on each ballot item.

- Use the spreadsheet function that calculates the Standard Deviation of the votes for each ballot item. Sort the ballot items in descending order by standard deviation.

CrowBar in GroupSystems

- Display voting results in the Vote or Alternative Analysis tool.

- In Vote: GroupSystems displays the standard deviation for the votes of each ballot item. You can sort the results in descending order by standard deviation.

- In Alternative Analysis: GroupSystems calculates a statistic called "Coefficient of Concordance." It's related to standard deviation. The results for ballot items with a coefficient of concordance above a certain threshold display with a green background. The results for a ballot item with coefficient of concordance below the threshold display with a green background. You can set the threshold to whatever level you want between zero and one. Adjust the threshold so that there are approximately as many items with a red background as you could expect to get through in the time allotted. For example, if you were to allot 30 minutes to the Crowbar, you might set the threshold so the six or seven most contentious items display with a red background. Sort ballot items in descending order by standard deviation or coefficient of concordance.

EXECUTION RULES

The following rules have to be followed while performing the CrowBar thinkLet:

- Assign speaking turns to participants to explain a voting score rather than letting participants volunteer to speak.

- Alternate between asking an explanation for a high score and an explanation for a low score.

- Do not allow participants to argue with each other immediately. Just ask for explanations of both sides of the argument before letting a free discussion take place so that relevant insights have been made explicit.

- Always keep the discussion focused on a single ballot item. Conclude the discussion before moving to the next item on the list.

SAMPLE SCRIPT

The following is a sample script that lets you execute the above rules and perform the CrowBar thinkLet:

Say This

1. *"The items near the bottom of the list are the ones upon which you have the most agreement."*

2. *"However, you do not have consensus about the items near the top of the list."*

3. *"Let's consider this first item. Some of you rated it quite high, while others of you rated it quite low."*

4. *"Let's start with you, <Name participant>. Without telling me how you voted, what reasons might exist for rating <this ballot item> on <the polling criterion>, and what reasons might exist for rating <this ballot item> low on <the polling criterion>"?*

Do This

5. Moderate a discussion about what reasons might exist for high and low ratings of an item. Repeat the CrowBar prompt any time the discussion seems to stray.

6. Ask for responses from several group members. Repeat the full CrowBar prompt for each person you ask.

7. If you get many responses on one side of the issue (e.g. why people gave high ratings), then repeat the prompt asking for reasons that may exist for the opposite ratings (e.g. "What reasons might exist for giving <this ballot

item> a low rating?).

8. Keep track of and periodically repeat the reasons the group suggests on each side of the issue.

9. Repeat this process for any ballot item that seem worthy of such discussion.

Consider This

10. To move the group towards consensus on a final score for a ballot item, consider using the MoodRing thinkLet during or immediately after the CrowBar discussion on each item.

INSIGHTS

Essence (How it works)

The most essential element of the Crowbar thinkLet lies in the prompt, "without telling me how you voted, what reasons might exist…" Some surprising things happen when you prompt the group in this way. First the discussion tends to keep a laser-like focus on the issue at hand. Even in emotionally charged situations, we see little of the digression and off-topic wanderings that are typical of unstructured discussions. We also spend much less time arguing in violent agreement with one another.

Effects

Crowbar is one of the thinkLets we use most frequently in our work with teams. It is very simple, yet it is intense and powerful. During the discussion, all sorts of useful interesting things are revealed. People express and examine assumptions they didn't even realize they were making. They often share information that the rest of the group didn't know. Sometimes they reveal their hidden agendas, which lets the group move to address them much more directly as they move forward. Occasionally they discover ambiguities in a ballot item. Sometimes they even find that someone misunderstood the evaluation criteria.

During a Crowbar, people not only reveal assumptions about the issues under consideration, they also reveal assumptions (often mistaken) about people who voted differently than they did. Thus, the Crowbar can be a useful tool for helping team members learn about one another's needs and motivations. As such it has been a useful team-building tool.

Why it works

The phrase, "Without telling me how you voted…" lets people articulate a position without having to be seen as endorsing the idea. It works as a safety net. The phrase "What reasons could exist…" keeps the conversation very focused. People are considering what reasons they or others could have for their votes. It lets people voice suspicions without appearing hostile. It lets them defend their positions without seeming combative. The repetition of the ballot item and the polling criterion with each prompt keeps the conversation focused on the specific issue at hand. It reminds people what they are to talk about, and keeps them from straying to irrelevant topics.

Although you prompt the participants not to tell you how they voted, people very often choose to abandon their anonymity and say things like, "Well, I voted such-and-such because…" Don't let that trouble you, and don't bother to enforce it. If someone claims a position aloud, it means they are not concerned about having to endorse it, so there is no negative consequence for group dynamics.

For these reasons, we suggest you quickly get in the habit of repeating <u>both</u> the ballot item the voting criteria *twice* in every crowbar prompt, just as it is framed in Step 4 of the script above. Pay careful attention to the wording. It really helps keep the discussion focused. For example:

- "Without telling me how you voted, what reasons might exist for somebody to say that it was critical to keep football at this school, and what reasons might exist for to say that football is useless at this school?"
- "Without telling me how you voted, what reasons might exist for somebody to say that implementing an ERP is very important, and what reasons might exist for saying that implementing an ERP is very unimportant?
- "…what reasons might exist for saying that our competitor's new product is a major threat, and what reasons might exist for saying that the competitor's product is a minor threat?"
- "…what reasons might exist for rating this vendor as superior, and what reasons might exist for rating this vendor as inferior?"

Pitfalls

<u>Domination</u>. Research shows that, without intervention, the most vocal speaker in a group takes about 1/3 the airtime. The next-most vocal person takes about 1/3 of what's left, and so on down to the person who says nothing. This can be particularly problematic in a Crowbar activity with a participant who wants to advocate for

his or her own position without bothering to learn about the assumptions, preferences, or information held by others in the group .

You can mitigate domination by giving the Crowbar prompt to specific people in the group instead of asking for responses from volunteers. This will bring out insights from people who have lower status or who prefer not to volunteer answers for other reasons. If you have a person who still insists on dominating, you may mitigate the problem by the following procedure:

- Make and hold eye contact with the dominant speaker.
- Move sufficiently close to the person that you make a small violation of their personal space.
- Ask the person to summarize their position succinctly, to clarify it for the group
- Repeat the person's position back to them in your own words to demonstrate that you heard and understood.
- Staying close to the dominator, turn your back to face the rest of the group, saying, "OK, thanks for that contribution…." Then give the Crowbar prompt to another person. This approach usually mitigates the domination problem.

Impasse. Often, the Crowbar is sufficient to resolve disagreements. People will reconsider their assumptions, share information, agree on definitions of terms, change their goals, or compromise on their preferences. However, sometimes a crowbar reveals a genuine impasse, where it becomes clear that group members have sound reasons for holding mutually exclusive positions. In such cases, the Crowbar, having served its purpose, is no longer useful. Consider moving the issue into another consensus-building activity like PointCounterPoint, which produces potential solutions.

SUCCESS STORY

We once worked on a strategic plan with 8 members of the senior management council for a consulting firm that was fighting for survival in a rapidly changing market. By the time we joined the process, the two partners in the firm, who had the highest personal esteem for one another, were nonetheless in a painful conflict about the future directions of the firm. One, who was near retirement age, seemed to be far more risk averse than the other, who was in mid-career.

When we began work, the two partners took seats on opposite sides at opposite ends of the table. This was not a good sign. We began work by asking the team to FreeBrainstorm strategic initiatives that the firm could undertake. We FastFocused the initiatives to a StrawPoll ballot and ask the participants to rate each initiative on a scale from 1 to 10 for its importance to the long-term survival of the company. When the results were sorted by Standard deviation, it was immediately obvious that the group lacked consensus on one issue in particular. Two people had given the initiative a rating of 8; the rest had given it ratings of 3 or 4.

We gave the Crowbar prompt:

"Without telling me how you voted, what reasons might exist for saying this initiative is vital to the long term survival of the company, and what reasons might exist for saying this is unimportant to the long term survival of the company?"

The group seemed to hold its breath, as if waiting for the other shoe to drop. Finally, with obvious reluctance, one of the partners said:

"I gave this initiative an 8. Of all the ideas on the table, this is the most important…"

He began to recite the arguments and reasons for his vote. His partner sat open mouthed with astonishment. When he finally got his turn to speak he said:

"You gave that an 8? I'm the other person who gave it an 8. It's absolutely mandatory that we implement this initiative immediately."

He recited his supporting arguments, which were quite different than those of the other partner. When he was done speaking, the two partners rose spontaneously from their chairs and circled the table to embrace one another. They sat down together at the head of the table. It turned out indeed had been more risk averse than the other, but they had been talking about different initiatives without realizing it, one wanting to take a risk on one initiative, the other wanting to be conservative on another. They had also been using the same words for different concepts. The Crowbar discussion surfaced all these issues and the firm was able to move forward in unity.

Chapter Seven

Collaboration Technology

A Taxonomy of Collaboration Technologies

Once upon a time the authors of this book worked with the headquarters staff of a large organization with world-wide presence. The organization's charter required that it develop creative, cross-disciplinary solutions to fast-breaking opportunities and challenges in its volatile operating environment. The best of these solutions seemed to emerge from a fluid, open exchange of the rich experiences and knowledge of the headquarters' 500+ knowledge workers. Yet the organization seemed bound in an outdated, multi-layered bureaucracy that was insufficiently responsive to the accelerating pace of change in their environment. The consultants were chartered to help the organization develop a more effective work practice for conducting their weekly staff meetings. Hundreds of staff meetings took place every week to provide management status updates for current projects. The staff complained of the stultifying, painful nature of these meetings, which typically involved about ten people and lasted about two hours. The organization had a culturally ingrained practice of presenting from PowerPoint slides at these meetings, and the meeting was usually the first time group members saw each other's' slides. Knowledge workers briefed their managers; managers briefed executives; and executives briefed senior executives up through the top levels of leadership. Management wanted a system that would allow people to preview status presentations before the meeting so that more attention could be paid to generating creative solutions that added value to the organization.

The consultants worked with stakeholders in the organization to develop five iterations of a new work practice for status reporting and creative problem solving. Each iteration used a different collaboration technology. The first implementation was pen-and-paper. We subsequently prototyped the process with a group support system, a shared document editor, a Wiki, and a web portal. Each iteration revealed new problems and constraints. The paper based system, for example did not provide shared access to critical information. The group support system provided shared access to information, but turned out to have unacceptable constraints on access controls. Its tools were well suited to in-meeting interactions, but were not as useful for between-meeting interactions. The shared editor provided the right access controls, but lacked support for the variety of structures the group needed to create. The Wiki provided for the variety of structures, but did not provide the requisite synchronicity for certain user actions. The web portal provided sufficient access controls, support for between-meeting coordination, variety of structures, and synchronicity of actions. Lacking a systematic way to analyze and articulate collaboration needs and to select among the many groupware possibilities, the evolution through these prototypes required more than a year.

The scope of this problem becomes more apparent when one considers that the rise of the global marketplace and the advancing of the World Wide Web have given impetus to rapid advances in groupware technologies and products. Today, hundreds of new groupware products exist to support collaboration by work teams, with more appearing monthly. This recent growth in the groupware marketplace is driven by the need for organizations to adapt to the rapidly-changing global business environment (Watson-Manheim et al., 2002) and enabled by the maturation of Web2.0 development techniques (e.g. AJAX and Ruby on Rails). Online meeting collaboration and virtual project management are increasingly common modes of work as teams operate more and more frequently across departmental, organizational, and geographic boundaries to innovate and create value (see e.g. Nunamaker et al., 2001; Evans & Wolf, 2005; Munkvold & Zigurs, 2005).

Commercial vendors tend to sculpt niches in the marketplace by bundling mixes of core technologies. For example, the most recent version of Yahoo Messenger has basic instant message functionality, along with file exchange, and audio conferencing, which are distinctly different core technologies and yet are packaged under a single "instant messaging" label. These "bundles of capabilities" – collaboration suites in a realm with no traditional or commonly accepted product categories or commonly accepted capability feature sets – make it difficult for practitioners to understand what capabilities they need, what capabilities a given product offers, and to select an appropriate groupware product for their mix of tasks (DeSanctis & Poole, 1994; Zigurs & Khazanchi, *in press*). The rapid elaboration of the groupware space also raises complexity for groupware researchers to make sense of what value can be created with current technologies, how and why such value can be created, and what groupware challenges still remain unaddressed.

Journalists and bloggers offer several approaches to categorizing collaboration products, each of which is useful to its purposes (e.g., http://www.collaboration-tools.com/,http://itredux.com/office-20/database/, and http://www.solutionwatch.com/515/back-to-school-with-the-class-of-web-20-part-2/). More formal typologies have appeared over years of research, from the classic "time-place" classification of technologies (Nunamaker et al., 1991; Poltrock & Grudin, 1994) to early schemes that grouped technologies according to whether they are communications- or process-oriented (Pinsonneault & Kraemer, 1989). Later schemes further decomposed process-oriented technologies to accommodate information processing and overall group process perspectives (Zigurs & Buckland, 1998). Despite these incremental improvements, a simple, relatively stable, and comprehensive taxonomic model of elemental collaboration technologies has not yet emerged.

In this chapter, based on the work of Mittleman, Briggs, Murphy, & Davis (2009), we propose a starting place toward developing such a model. The purpose of this classification scheme is to provide a lens through which people can better understand the capabilities of, and relationships between, collaboration technologies. Such a framework might then help practitioners to select from among commercial collaboration software offerings, offer groupware designers a range of design choices for new systems, and reveal new challenges to the groupware research community. This chapter starts by describing the overall process used to gather and analyze the data necessary to develop the scheme. Next, it develops a comparison scheme that formed the basis by which collaboration products were grouped. An initial classification scheme for collaboration technologies is then presented. The chapter concludes with examples of how to use the comparison and classification schemes, along with a discussion of potential directions for future research.

Scheme Development

Over the course of 5+ years a team of collaboration researchers has searched the commercial marketspace for new groupware products to develop the current listing of more than 250 products. Throughout that timeframe, the team has analyzed those products to derive factors that could be used to classify those products. As new products emerge, the team regularly re-examined the scheme to assess fit. This inductive process, driven by actual collaboration tools in use in the marketplace, drove the derivation of the original scheme and continues to shape it as collaboration products develop.

Initial analysis revealed that it would not be possible to create a taxonomy for groupware *products* because products tend to be heavily-overlapping bundles of *technologies* rather than distinguishable, classifiable entities. We define a groupware technology as a software solution which, if implemented, could help move a group toward its goals in some specific way. We define a collaboration product as an implementation of one or more collaboration technologies offered as an integrated package.

Therefore the products were re-analyzed to distill from them to a set of the elemental collaboration capabilities that comprised them. Next the development of detailed functional descriptions of the products was required, and the descriptions were reviewed for accuracy and completeness. Then a set of key themes were distilled from those descriptions that characterize the attributes by with which one could compare different implementations of groupware technologies, both within and across categories. Three groupware experts were asked to apply the initial set of themes to the original functional descriptions to verify their completeness. We identified discrepancies, and refined the attribute set until the core set of attributes could be generally applied to any product in the set. The resultant comparison scheme is presented in Section Three.

The most critical attribute by which groupware products could be compared and contrasted was their fundamental technical capabilities. We therefore reexamined the groupware products to address the basic question, "What are the core underlying technologies represented in this constellation of products?" We organized the core technologies into a classification scheme with three main branches, which appears in Section Four.

Comparing Collaboration Technologies

The implementation of technologies and their details can vary from product to product. When comparing technologies, it is useful to sort out which affordances are present, which are absent, and which can be configured to adapt to variations of need. In this section, we draw attention to key attributes by which one can compare and contrast collaboration technologies when designing or selecting among collaboration products. The comparison scheme consists of nine architectural constructs for collaboration technology affordances including: 1) core functionality, 2) content, 3) relationships, 4) supported actions, 5) action parameters, 6) access control, 7) session persistence, 8) alert mechanisms, and 9) presence indicators. Table 1 lists these capabilities and briefly describes each attribute of the comparison scheme.

Table 1. Summary of the Comparison Scheme Attributes (Mittleman, Briggs, Murphy, & Davis, 2009).

Capability	Affordances essential to the nature of the technology
Core Functionality	Primary functionality provided by the tool. This maps to the tool's location within the classification scheme (see Table 2).
Content	Possible content for contributions to a collaboration system are: text, links, raster graphic, vector graphic, and data-stream.
Relationships	Users can establish these kinds of relationships among contributions: collection, list, tree, and network.
Supported Actions	Actions that users can take on structures or relations.
Add	Ability to create structures or relations.
Receive	Ability to receive, view, or read contributions to the system.
Associate	Establish relationships among contributions
Edit	Ability to modify content or relationships.
Move	Change relationships among contributions
Delete	Ability to eliminate content or relationships.
Judge	Render opinions on the relative merits of contributions
Action Parameters	Three key parameters that characterize or modify actions.
Synchronicity	Expected delay between the time one person executes an action and the time other users can perceive the effects of that action.
Identifiability	Degree to which users can determine who executed an action.
Access Controls	The granting or revoking of user ability to execute supported actions.
Session Persistence	The degree to which contributions are ephemeral or permanent.
Alert Mechanisms	The ways participants are notified that something or someone in the system requires their attention.
Presence Indicators	The means by which users may know what other users have access to a session, the nature of their roles, and their current status.

Core Functionality identifies the primary capability provided by a tool. The core capability of a *blog*, for example, is a page to which users may contribute shared text or hyperlinks to other pages (new posts). The core functionality of *voice conference* is a continuous audio stream. We discuss core capabilities in much more detail in Section Four, where we propose a classification scheme for collaboration technology.

Content describes the kinds of data that may be contributed to a particular collaboration (Briggs et al.,1997). These data structures include:

- *Text*: a block of textual information (e.g. a text message).

- *Links*: reference pointers with labels (e.g. a URL).

- *Raster Graphic*: pixel-based graphical representation (e.g. a jpg or gif picture).

- *Vector Graphic*: object and relation based graphical representation (e.g. a flow chart or an architectural drawing).

- *Data stream*: a continuous data flow (e.g. a sound channel or desktop sharing).

- *Hypermedia*: Combinations of the content types above.

Relationships are the associations users can establish among contributions. Four types of relationships are possible among contributions:

- *Collection*: connotes membership in a set of otherwise unrelated objects.

- *List*: a list an ordered set of objects (e.g. before/after, bigger/smaller).

- *Tree*: a set of objects in hierarchical relationships with each object (except the root) having only one parent, but having zero-to-many children (e.g. system, subsystem, component).

- *Network*: an organization where each object can have zero to many links to other objects (e.g. parents, siblings, children, cousins…).

Relationships may be established among objects of same or differing content. Tools may support only a single kind of relationship or may support several types. This variety enables a vast array of information constructions. Some groupware may articulate the semantics of the relationships represented in the content. Other tools only represent the syntax of relationships, leaving it up to group members to agree on semantics.

<u>Supported Actions</u> indicate the things a system allows participant to do to content and relationships. These actions (already well-established in the database and groupware literatures) are:

- *Add*: contribute content to the group (e.g. add a new item to a blog; speak during an audio conference).

- *Receive*: detect contributions made by self or others (e.g. view text contributions or hear an audio channel)

- *Associate*: establish relationships among contributions (e.g. organize ideas into categories or arrange content into an outline)

- *Edit*: modify content of a contribution (e.g. amend or change text already contributed to a session),

- *Move*: change relationships among contributions

- *Delete*: remove a contribution from a session (e.g. delete text, erase audio)

- *Judge*: render an opinion on the relative merits of contributions (e.g. vote).

<u>Action Parameters</u> describe characteristics of actions that impact user's experience of contributions and of one another when using a collaboration tool.

- *Synchronicity* characterizes expected delay between the time that a user executes an action and the time other users respond to that action. For example, with audio conferences, participants expect a response to their contributions within a second or two, whereas with e- mail, users expect that responses may be delayed by hours or days. In some systems (e.g. audio conferencing) participants must wait their turn to contribute and in others (e.g. group support systems, wikis) participants may contribute simultaneously.

- *Identifiability* characterizes the degree to which users can determine who executed an action.

- *Identifiability* ranges from full anonymity, to sub-group identification, to pseudonym identification (so you may know which contributions came from the same person, but not who that person is), to full identification.

Access Control deals with the configuration of user's rights and privileges with respect to entering a session and executing supported actions. Some actions may be always available (e.g. in an instant messaging, all users may always add), or always blocked (e.g. in instant messaging, no users may edit or delete contributions. Still others may be configurable on the fly (e.g. in some group support systems, anonymity may be switched on or off as needed).

Session Persistence is the degree to which contributions are ephemeral or permanent. In some collaboration tools (e.g. video or audio conferencing) contributions may be ephemeral, disappearing as soon as they are made. In others, contributions persist only for the duration of a session and disappear when all users exit (e.g. instant messaging). Often time users may configure the degree to which their contributions persist. For example, in some system users may decide whether session contents will be saved. Other systems (e.g. e-mail) allow a user to delete contributions from their view, but the contributions remain in the views of others, or in a permanent record.

Alert Mechanisms are the way participants are interrupted or notified that something in the system demands their attention. For example, instant messenger systems typically signal an arriving contribution by making a sound and popping up a momentary visual cue. The interrupt is designed to attract immediate attention; however, it can be ignored or refused by the receiver. Alerts, like those from an RSS feed, for example, do not interrupt the user but rather require that the user deliberately seek them out.

Awareness Indicators are the ways users learn about the other people who have access to a session, the roles that they hold, and their current status. In some systems, the only indicator that others are present is arrival of new contributions. In others, people may see a list of participants who have been granted access. In some, users can learn who is currently active in a session, what they are doing, which tools they are using, which contributions they are manipulating, and in some cases, even their current state of mind (e.g. happy, confused, dissatisfied).

The comparison scheme presented here draws our attention to key attributes by which one can compare, contrast, optimize, and select among groupware technology implementation. The most important of these attributes is the core capability, which we elaborate more fully in the next section.

A Classification Scheme for Collaboration Technologies

This section provides a finer-grained examination of the core capabilities in the form of a classification scheme for collaboration technologies. The first level of the classification scheme divides all collaboration technologies into four main categories according to their most-fundamental capabilities: 1) jointly authored pages, 2) streaming tools, 3) information access tools, and 4) aggregated systems. The fourth category is for technologies that must integrate a mix of tools from the first three categories and optimize them to support work practices that that cannot be achieved with a single technology. The scheme further subdivides each of the top four categories into sub- categories by the functions they are optimized to support (see Table 2). This section summarizes these categories and their subcategories.

Table 2: Summary of the Classification Scheme for Collaboration Technology (Mittleman et al., 2009)

Categories	Descriptions
Jointly Authored Pages	Technologies that provide one or more windows that multiple users may view, and to which multiple users may contribute, usually simultaneously.
Conversation Tools	Optimized to support dialog among group members.
Shared Editors	Optimized for the joint production of deliverables like documents, spreadsheets, or graphics.
Group Dynamics Tools	Optimized for creating, sustaining, or changing patterns of collaboration among people making joint effort toward a goal (e.g. idea generation, idea clarification, idea evaluation, idea organization, consensus-building).
Polling Tools	Optimized for gathering, aggregating, and understanding judgments, opinions, and information from multiple people.
Streaming Technologies	Technologies that provide a continuous feed of changing data.
Desktop / Application Sharing	Optimized for remote viewing and/or control of the computers of other group members.
Audio Conferencing	Optimized for transmission and receipt of sounds.
Video Conferencing	Optimized for transmission and receipt of dynamic images.
Information Access Tools	Technologies that provide group members with ways to store, share, find, and classify data objects.
Shared File Repositories	Provide group members with ways to store and share digital files.
Social Tagging Systems	Provide means to affix keyword tags to digital objects so that users can find objects of interest, and so they can find others with similar interests.
Search Engines	Provide means to retrieve relevant digital objects from among vast stores of objects based on search criteria.
Syndication Tools	Provide notification of when new contributions of interest have been added to pages or repositories.
Aggregated Systems	Technologies that combine of other technologies and tailor them to support a specific kind of task.

Jointly Authored Pages

The most fundamental capability for all technologies in the jointly authored pages category is a digital page, defined as a single window to which multiple collaborative participants can contribute, often simultaneously. The data structures of pages might include text, graphics, numbers, or other digital objects. However, regardless of content, any contribution made by a participant will generally appear on the screens of the other participants who view the same page. A given technology based on jointly authored pages may provide a single page or multiple pages. In some cases the contributions to one page serve as hyperlinks to other pages, allowing for the creation of hierarchies or networks of pages. Jointly authored pages are the basis for several sub-categories of collaboration technology including: conversation tools, shared editors, group dynamics tools, and polling tools.

Conversation Tools are those primarily optimized to support dialog among group members. Email is a widely-used conversation tool as well as short message services (SMS) (i.e. cell phone text messaging) which is becoming increasingly common. According to Verizon Wireless, their customers sent and received more than 10 billion text messages in June 2007 (Zeman, 2007). Other conversation tools include instant messaging, chat rooms, and blogs or threaded discussions. Instant messaging and chat rooms provide users with a single shared page to which they can contribute contributions to a chronologically ordered list. Participants may not move, edit, or delete their contributions. Instant messaging and chat rooms differ from one another only in their access and alert mechanisms. With instant messaging an individual receives a pop-up invitation that another individual wishes to hold a conversation, while with chat rooms an individual browses to a web site to find and join a conversation. Blogs (otherwise known as Web Logs) and threaded discussion tools are optimized for less-synchronous conversations. Users make a contribution, then come back later to see how others may have responded. Blogs and threaded discussions are typically persistent (i.e. their content remains even when users are not contributing) whereas chat rooms and instant messaging are usually ephemeral (i.e. when the last person exits a session, the session content disappears).

Shared Editor tools are typically a jointly authored page optimized for the creation of a certain kind of deliverable by multiple authors. The content and affordances of these tools often match those of single-user office suite tools (e.g. .word processing, spreadsheet); however they are enhanced to accept contributions and editing by multiple simultaneous users. A wiki (the Hawaiian word for 'fast') is another example of joint document authoring. Wikis are simple web pages that can be create directly through a web browser by any authorized user without the use of off-line web development tools.

Group Dynamics Tools are optimized for creating, sustaining, or changing patterns of collaboration among individuals making a joint effort toward a goal. The patterns these tools support include generating ideas, establishing shared understanding of them, converging on those worth more attention, organizing and evaluating ideas, and building consensus (Briggs et al., 2006). These tools are often implemented as multiple layers of jointly authored pages such that each contribution on a given page may serve as a hyperlink to a sub-page. The affordances of such tools are typically easily configurable, so at any given moment a group leader can provide team members with the features they need (e.g. view, add, move) while blocking features they should not be using (e.g. edit, delete).

Polling Tools are a special class of jointly authored pages, optimized for gathering, aggregating, and understanding judgments, or opinions from multiple people. At a minimum, the shared pages of a polling tool must offer a structure of one or more ballot items, a way for users to record votes, and a way to display results. Polling tools may offer rating, ranking, allocating, or categorizing evaluation methods and may also support the gathering of text based responses to ballot items.

Streaming Technologies

The core capability of all tools in the streaming technologies category is a continuous feed of dynamic data. Desktop sharing, application sharing, and audio/video conferencing are common examples of streaming technologies

Desktop and Application Sharing Tools allow the events displayed on one computer to be seen on the screens of other computers. With some application sharing tools, members may use their own mouse and keyboard to control the remotely viewed computer.

Audio Conferencing Tools provide a continuous channel for multiple users to send and receive sound while Video Conferencing Tools allow users to send and receive sound or moving images. Typically all users may receive contributions in both types of tools, however systems may vary in the mechanisms they provide for alerts and access control as well as by the degree to which affordances can be configured and controlled by a leader.

Information Access Technologies

Information access technologies provide ways to store, share, classify, and find data and information objects. Key examples from this category are shared file repositories, social tagging, search engines, and syndication tools.

Shared File Repositories provide mechanisms for group members to store digital files where others in the group can access them. Some such systems also provide version control mechanisms such as check-out, check-in capabilities, and version back-ups.

Social Tagging allows users to affix keyword tags to digital objects in a shared repository. For example, the web site, del.icio.us allows users to store and tag their favorite web links (i.e. bookmarks) online so they can access them from any computer. Users are not only able to access their own bookmarks by keyword, but bookmarks posted and tagged by others as well. More significantly, users can find other users who share an interest in the same content. Social tagging systems allow for the rapid formation of communities of interest and communities of practice around the content of the data repository. The data in a social tagging repository are said be organized in a folksonomy, an organization scheme that emerges organically from the many ways that users think of and tag contributions, rather than a taxonomy, organized by experts.

Search Engines use search criteria provided by users to retrieve digital objects from among vast stores of such objects (e.g. the Worldwide Web, the blogosphere, digital libraries). Search criteria may include content, tags, and other attributes of the objects in the search space. Some search engines interpret the semantic content of the search request to find related content that is not an exact match for the search criteria.

Syndication tools allow a user to receive a notification when new contributions to pages or repositories they deem to be of interest (e.g. blogs, wikis, and social networks). Users subscribe to receive update alerts from a feed on a syndicated site. Every time the site changes, the feed broadcasts an alert message to all its subscribers. Users view alerts using software called an aggregator. Any time a user opens their aggregator, they see which of their subscription sites has new contributions. Therefore, users do not need to scan all contents to discover new contributions.

Aggregated Technologies

Aggregated technologies integrate several technologies from the other three categories and optimize them to support a task that cannot be executed using a single technology (DeSanctis & Poole, 1994). Aggregated technologies deliver value which could be achieved with a collection of stand-alone tools. There are many examples of aggregated technologies, among them virtual workspaces, group support systems, and social networking systems. Virtual workspaces often combine document repositories, team calendars, conversation tools and other technologies that make it easier for team members to execute coordinated efforts (e.g. Groove or SharePoint). Remote presentation or web conferencing systems often combine application sharing and audio streams with document repositories and polling tools optimized to support one-to-many broadcast of presentations, with some ability for the audience to provide feedback to the presenter (e.g. WebEx or SameTime). Group support systems integrate collections of group dynamics tools to move groups seamlessly through a series of activities toward a goal, for example, by generating ideas in one tool, organize them in another, and evaluating them in yet another (e.g. GroupSystems or WebIQ). Social networking systems (e.g. MySpace or Flickr) combine social tagging with elements of wikis, blogs, other shared page tools, and a search engine so users can find and communicate with their acquaintances as well as establish new relationships based on mutual friends or mutual interests. Thus, aggregated technologies may combine any mix shared-page, streaming, and information access technologies to support a particular purpose.

Summary

In this chapter we present the comparison and classification schemes as the starting place toward a taxonomy of collaboration technology. One can use the classification scheme to analyze, compare, and contrast the capabilities offered by groupware products. Additionally, one can use the comparison scheme to compare and contrast important implementation choices in technologies within the same category or across categories.

Example Use of the Comparison and Classification Schemes

Table 3 illustrates how the comparison scheme can be used to weight the capabilities of two collaboration technologies (i.e. instant messaging and video conferencing) against each other.

Table 3. Example of the Comparison Scheme Attributes (Mittleman et al., 2009).

Attribute	Instant messaging	Video Conferencing
Core Functionality	Creation and exchange of single text pages	Single video stream, usually paired with a single audio stream
Content	Text	A/V streams
Relationships	Time-ordered list of text contributions	Time-ordered sequence of synchronized sounds and images
Supported Actions		
Add/	Text	Audio and Video in parallel;
Receive/	Yes	Yes
Associate	No	No
Edit	No	No
Move	No	No
Delete	No	No
Judge	No	No
Action Parameters		
Synchronicity	Immediate display of contributions to all participants; users may add content in parallel	Immediate presentation of all contributions to all participants; users will add content in parallel
Identifiability	Identification of contributor by login-name is automatic and mandatory	Identification of contributor typically only by cues embedded into the stream (e.g. sound of voice, face recognition)
Access Control	Receive by invitation only. Once invitation is accepted, all users have both add and receive rights	Varies by system. Access ranges from browsing to dial-up access. Control ranges from open to password or access code. Once in, all users have view rights. Add rights may be under the control of a moderator
Session Persistence	For duration of session by default; manual or automatic saving optional	For the duration of session by default; manual or automatic saving optional
Alert Mechanisms	Interrupt by invitation with sound, pop up visual cue	Vary by system, ranging e-mail invitations, to audio and visual interrupts

Note that any given implementation of IM or video conferencing system could differ from these configurations in many ways and still be essentially the same class of technology. The differences, though, could have significant impact on the degree to which the implementation serves the needs of the users. To better illustrate this point, consider the following scenario. One of this paper's authors was consulted about a technology selection by a systems integrator who operates out of the Midwest United States to service customers nationwide. They had selected MS- LiveMeeting® as the technology platform for conducting a distributed requirements elicitation for a product under development. Without knowing anything more about the situation, the author predicted that the chosen solution would be ineffective. He was able to make that judgment based on the fact that he knew that though LiveMeeting was quite capable as a streaming technology, it lacked key technical features found in jointly authored page and information access categories that would also be important for the success of the project. This scenario demonstrated how basic knowledge of the classification scheme can help assess potential technical solutions.

Implications and Future Research

The goal in presenting these comparison and classification schemes was to address the challenge of understanding and selecting among various collaboration technologies. Additionally, the scheme can be used to identify new opportunities for collaboration technologies by identifying gaps or holes where technology was not offered.

We have found that even this first version significantly reduced cognitive load for understanding the broad groupware space. It has its limitations, particularly in terms of accommodating the aggregated products. However, the classification and comparison schemes represent a credible step forward that may help groupware researchers, designers, and users to analyze and understand the sometimes complex "bundles of capabilities" found in collaboration products. The schemes may also help researchers and designers to understand the range of implementation choices available to them, and may help researchers to discover a) which of the many technological interventions account for effects observed in the field, and b) what groupware challenges remain unaddressed. We anticipate that further research will be required making additions and revisions to the schemes to bring them to a state where they can account for all elemental collaboration technologies and all design and configuration choices for those technologies.

Chapter Eight

Group Support Systems

It has been over two decades since Group Support Systems (GSS) emerged on the Information Technology (IT) scene. GSS are defined as socio-technical systems consisting of software, hardware, meeting procedures, facilitation support, and a group of meeting participants engaged in intellectual collaborative work (Briggs, de Vreede, Vogel, Kolfschoten, & Wien, 2003). A GSS can radically change the dynamics of group interactions by improving communication, by structuring and focusing problem solving efforts, and by establishing and maintaining an alignment between personal and group goals. A GSS can also reduce cognitive costs of communication and information access among teams working collaboratively towards a goal. A GSS provides high customizability and easily maps to different interfaces.

Specifically, a GSS is a collection of collaborative meeting tools designed to improve creative problem solving by teams (Briggs & de Vreede, 1997). A GSS is typically based on a network of personal computers, usually one for each participant. Sometimes participants work in meeting rooms especially designed for electronically supported meetings (see Figures 1, 2, & 3). These facilities often have carefully arranged seating and lighting, and one or more large public display screens. Other times the participants simply move laptop computers into a standard meeting room and begin their work. Still other times, participants work from their offices, coordinating their GSS efforts via voice links and e-mail.

A GSS permits all participants to *speak at once* by typing their ideas into the system. The system immediately makes all contributions available to the other participants on their screens. Nobody has to wait for a turn to speak, so people don't forget what they want to say while waiting for the floor. People don't forget what has been said, because there is an electronic record of the conversation on their screens. They can stop to think without losing the thread of the meeting.

GSS also allows a group to enter ideas anonymously, when it is appropriate. During the generation phase of creativity it is often useful to get every idea on the table, but people often hold back unconventional or unpopular ideas for fear of disapproval from peers or superiors. The anonymity of the GSS allows the ideas to surface without fear of repercussion. Further, because the ideas are anonymous, the team can only evaluate them on their merits, rather than their source. In labor management negotiations, for example, it is often difficult for an idea to receive a fair hearing, because if it is proposed by one side it is immediately suspect by the other. Anonymous teamwork can help overcome such impasses.

Figure 1 A Group Support System.
(de Vreede, 2010).

Used in face-to-face mode on a standard conference table. Participants contribute through parallel electronic channels in addition to regular channels.

Figure 2. GSS Research Laboratory.
(de Vreede, 2010).

Figure 3. Large Facilitation Session Supported by GSS.
(de Vreede, 2010).

GSS Software

Each tool in a GSS toolkit focuses and structures the thinking of the team in some unique way (Briggs & de Vreede, 1997). An electronic brainstorming tool, for example, is designed to intentionally fragment a group's thinking and prevent them going into depth on any one topic. This kind of tool encourages them to diverge from comfortable thinking patterns, to seek farther and farther afield for new ideas. An idea organizer, on the other hand, encourages a group to converge very quickly on a few key issues. A topic-commenting tool encourages the team to explore ideas in great depth and detail. See Table 1 for a summary of tools in GroupSystems for Windows.

> **Table 1. A Summary of Tools in GroupSystems for Windows.**
> Adapted from Briggs & de Vreede (1997).
>
> **Electronic Brainstorming** allows rapid generation of a free flow of ideas.
>
> **Topic Commenter** permits people to generate ideas and assign them to "file folders" or topics.
>
> **Categorizer** gives structured methods for generating, synthesizing, and categorizing ideas.
>
> **Group Outliner** allows a group to explore issues and develop action plans using a tree or outline structure.
>
> **Alternative Analyzer** compares a set of alternatives against a set of group-developed criteria.
>
> **Vote** helps evaluate ideas, measure consensus, and make choices using several voting methods.
>
> **Survey** allows the group to respond to a questionnaire.
>
> **Briefcase** provides a set of personal productivity tools, including Calendar, File Reader, Notepad, Calculator, Clipboard and Quick Vote.

Other GSS tools, such as electronic polling, provide a variety of ways to measure group consensus -- rank ordering, weighting, agree-disagree, multiple selection, pair wise comparison, and others. Electronic polling turns out to be a superb method for opening discussions that have become stalled. Once people have registered their opinions, the leader can focus discussion by saying, "I see six people have rated Item 7 as most important, while four have rated it least important. Without telling me how you voted, can you tell me reasons that might exist for voting each way on this issue?" Subsequent conversation is usually most illuminating. It often turns out that people use different words for the same idea, or have different meanings for the same word. Sometimes people hold information that others do not know. Other times fundamental differences in assumptions surface. Groups often vote at the beginning of a discussion, and re-vote periodically to see how they are doing.

Making Sense of the Buzzwords

Over the last decade developers have created a new class of software aimed at making groups more productive. The umbrella term for this software was coined in 1981 by Peter and Trudy Johnson-Lenz: Groupware. Group Support Systems are but one kind of groupware. They differ substantially from systems like

Lotus Notes, which provides e-mail, team databases and computer conferencing systems. Where Lotus notes supports coordinated-but-independent team work, a GSS supports a concerted effort toward a plan-of-action. Where Lotus Notes offers a platform upon which any number of group tools could be built, a GSS is a set of finished applications, crafted to structure and focus group dynamics. Indeed, one could build a GSS on top of Lotus Notes, but Notes is not, in and of itself, a GSS.

GSS are now beginning to make their way from the laboratory into the workplace. As they do, a dizzying array of buzzwords float around them (Briggs & de Vreede, 1997). Originally GSS were called GDSS, or Group Decision Support System. Over time people came to realize that these systems supported much more of the team process than just decision making, and so the D was dropped. Another term, electronic meeting system (EMS) is synonymous with GSS. The term EMS appears more in trade literature, while the term GSS tends to be confined to the academic literature. Table 2 presents a host of other terms that surround GSS. Each has somewhat different connotations depending on the interests of those who coined the terms. Nonetheless Table 2 can serve as a Rosetta Stone for those interested in finding further information on the topic.

Table 2. Acronyms and Buzzwords surrounding Group Support Systems. (Briggs & de Vreede, 1997)	
CAC	Computer Assisted Communication
CC	Computer Conferencing
CIS	Communication Information System
CMCS	Computer Mediated Communication Support
CS	Collaborative Systems
CSCW	Computer Supported Cooperative Work
CWSS	Collaborative Work Support System
DGSS	Distributed Group Support Systems
EC	Electronic Communities
EMS	Electronic Meeting System
GCSS	Group Communication Support System
GDSS	Group Decision Support System
GIS	Group Information System.
GNSS	Group Negotiation Support Systems
TC	TeleCollaboration

Experiences from the Field

More than two million people world-wide have now participated in GSS-supported meetings. Table 3 shows a small sample of the variety of tasks for which the technology has been used. Table 3 presents a list of some of the organizations now using GSS on a regular basis. Rigorous studies documenting the results of thousands of cases show that teams using GSS to support creative problem-solving routinely report labor cost reductions averaging 50% and reductions of project calendar days averaging 90% (see e.g. Grohowski, et al., 1988; Post, 1992). How does one account for such gains? A GSS provides support to a team along four fundamental dimensions: communication, deliberation, information access, and goal congruence.

Table 3. A selection of Organizations Now using GSS on a Regular Basis
(Briggs & de Vreede, 1997; www.groupsystems.com, 2011)

Agilent Technologies	Lloyds Bank
American Airlines	Ministry of Housing and Spatial Planning,
Amsterdam Municipal Police Force	NASA
AT&T	NATO
Bell South	Netherlands
Bellcore	Nationale Nederlanden Insurances, Netherlands
Booz Allen Hamilton	Nokia
British Steel	Oticon Corporation
Chevron Pipeline	Procter & Gamble
Department of Transportation	Royal Dutch Telecom (KPN)
District of Columbia Public Schools	Sun Microsystems
Dyntek	Unisys
Environmental Protection Agency	U.S. Army
IBM	U.S. Marine Corps
Johns Hopkins University	U.S. Navy
Intel Corporation	Verizon Communications

Communication Support

Consider first the communication possible with a GSS. In a face-to-face meeting everybody must wait for a turn to speak. Available air-time must be divided among all participants who wish to speak. When a GSS is added to the environment, participants may speak aloud if they wish, but when everybody wants the floor at once, they may use the GSS to achieve *parallel communication*. They do not have to listen to others before they can submit their own views. Participants do not have to remember their ideas and criticisms until they have the floor and can therefore spend more time on generating new ideas. Teams using electronic brainstorming are able to produce many more unique ideas of higher quality than teams working without electronic support (Dennis et al. 1991; Valacich et al., 1994).

A team communicating in parallel can cover a great deal of ground in a very short time. It takes no longer to hear from everybody in the group than it does to hear from one person. However, this degree of productivity can have a down-side. A group of 15 people working for 40 minutes can easily produce 600 to 1000 lines of text. Special tools and techniques are required to prevent information overload. These will be addressed in the section on Deliberation Support.

A GSS also allows for *anonymous communication*. Studies have shown that during idea generation activities people generate many more ideas and of higher quality if they are allowed to contribute anonymously. People need not worry about the political implications of disagreeing with others, or floating ideas that do not conform to the main-stream world view. Anonymity allows participants to criticize ideas without criticizing the people who produced them. Studies have shown that identified groups produce fewer ideas when criticism is allowed, but anonymous groups produce more when criticism is allowed (Connolly et al., 1990). People explore the ideas without becoming bogged down by slighted egos.

On the other hand, anonymity is not an unmixed blessing. Many studies have shown that people exert less effort when they are anonymous than when they are identified. Steps can be taken to raise the effort made by anonymous workers. Moreover, people may be unwilling to share their best ideas with the rest of the group if they feel they will not get the credit for it. Also, while anonymity is useful during the idea generation phase, on some occasions it may hinder subsequent work. People who submit information anonymously may be reluctant to reveal their identity later. There have been cases where this left a group unclear about the meaning accuracy of the information. In some instances they have even deleted information that turned out to be pertinent (Vreede & Sol 1994). Further, there are times in a meeting when it is important for participants to take responsibility, to commit to action, and to commit resources. A leader must therefore use anonymity judiciously, as a tool, not as a

118

panacea.

When first faced with the concept of GSS, some have argued that it be a poor communication medium, asserting that text-based electronic communication lacks *social cues*, the subtle nuances of behavior and tone-of-voice that make face-to-face oral communication so rich. They point out, for example, that it is difficult to tell sarcasm from serious discussion in a computer conversation. A typical comment is, "I don't want to talk to a computer, I want to talk to my colleagues." However, bringing a GSS into a meeting does not eliminate any traditional meeting media. People may still speak, gesture, draw on whiteboards, pound on tables, and the like, and they can also work on-line. Rather than subtracting richness, the GSS provides yet another channel. When working on the GSS the participants do not engage the computer, they engage one another. The GSS gives the team more control over the richness of their media, providing orderly, anonymous, parallel communication when it is useful, but allowing free-form nose-to-nose argument when that is called for. Our experiences with teams using GSS show that they typically spend about half their time working on-line and the other half in oral discussion. Therefore, the leader and the team must choose to use the technology when it can benefit, and not use it when it would interfere.

Deliberation Support

GSS tools can often improve a group's deliberation processes as they struggle to make sense of their problems and plan their actions. The fundamental behaviors a group can execute in pursuit of their goals are a) generate ideas, b) organize ideas, and c) evaluate ideas. Subtle differences in a GSS interface can lead to substantial differences in group dynamics. During a generation task, for example, it may be important to push a group to diverge, to push beyond their normal thinking patterns. An electronic brainstorming tool provides each participant with a different electronic page. The system allows them to enter only a single, short idea before it randomly sends their page to another participant and randomly brings them a page containing someone else's idea. Such a tool fosters as many different simultaneous conversations as there are people in the room.

An electronic brainstorming tool provides a good mechanism for reducing information overload faced by large groups. For each new person added to the group, the system adds a new electronic page. Thus, no matter how large the group becomes, no single page becomes excessively full of ideas. When it comes time to converge on a list of key issues, the group can work in parallel, each participant working from a single page. Key issues presented on that page can be moved to a group list. Participants can exchange pages several times to assure completeness. Hence, key issues are identified with a minimum of cognitive load on the participants

In contrast to electronic brainstorming, a topic commenting tool provides the group with a pre-set list of topics, but allows them to explore each topic in as much detail and depth as they wish. Such a tool fosters a very different group dynamic than electronic brainstorming. Idea organizing tools typically allow a group to rapidly converge on a list of key issues from the unstructured, unfocused text of their free-form brainstorming. At each phase of the problem solving process the leader must choose the tool that best moves the group from where they are to where they need to be next.

Information Support

Every phase of the thinking process (idea generation, idea organization, and idea evaluation) requires *information gathering*. A GSS can improve information access by enabling larger groups and by creating a group memory. Using a GSS a team of 24 can work with the same dynamics as a group of five. Because large meetings can be effective, many more people can be included in a process. Researchers in the field have observed that GSS groups have many fewer instances of breaking off a meeting because people holding key information were not present. This factor accounts for a large percentage of the reduction in project days.

All ideas, comments, and votes that are entered during a meeting are stored electronically, creating a *group memory*. The results of previous meetings are readily available when a group reconvenes, or when another group tackles a similar problem. For instance, one avionics manufacturer was having a serious quality control problem. They searched their electronic meeting transcripts for the previous two years for further information. They discovered that there had never been a meeting to deal with this particular problem, but that it had come up in 19 other meetings. Further, in every case the products of one particular vendor were mentioned in connection with the problem. Armed with the record, they approached the vendor and resolved the quality problem.

Electronic group memory differs from `traditional' minutes in several important aspects (Culnan & Markus, 1987). First, as minutes are traditionally written by a single individual, they are likely to reflect that individual's understanding of the meeting outcome. The electronically generated group memory gives an objective history. Second, minutes do not often describe the participant's initial positions or their interim postures. Group memory depicts the evolution of the group's position over time. Finally, group memory makes each comment during a meeting public, to which others can refer at a later stage.

On the other side of the coin, the amount of information may become so large that special support is necessary to retrieve the relevant pieces of information. Furthermore, people may hesitate to contribute to electronic transcripts if everything is permanent. Some teams working on sensitive issues prefer not to have their processes documented. Such teams often delete their sessions as soon as they finish work. One military organization went as far as to physically shred a hard disk at the conclusion of an important session. However, other teams have used the group memory to document the validity of their deliberations. One university, feeling sensitive to issues of affirmative action, conducted all hiring decision making on line to prove that bias was not a part of their decision making.

Alignment of Goals

People always bring personal goals into a team effort. The team can only be productive to the degree that the goals of the team are congruent with the goals of the individuals on the team. Over the long term, people will not work against their perceived self-interest. There are a number of features and functions in an electronic meeting system that encourage the alignment of group and individual goals. Some tools permit anonymous input, which encourages people to speak up immediately if they perceive their ox is about to be gored. Because larger numbers of people can work together effectively, the whole group can learn about individual constraints early in the process, rather than having concerns fester under the surface, only to bring a project down after the investment of much time and expense. Some EMS tools specifically ask team members to identify the stakeholders in a project and to explicitly state their assumptions about each of them. This activity often surfaces misconceptions and unrealistic expectations, permitting a re-alignment of group and individual goals.

Group Size

It is important to select the GSS technology appropriate to the group. There is some evidence that groups larger than seven or eight people benefit more from electronic brainstorming than do smaller groups (Dennis, 1994). In real life settings, technology may be the only way to bring a very large, diverse group. The Jimmy Carter Foundation in Atlanta, Georgia, used a GSS to support a meeting of more than 200 people from all sectors of the community, from bank presidents to homeless people. The group generated ideas to improve economic and social conditions in the community.

Groups with more diversity of knowledge and experience also benefit more from electronic brainstorming than groups where everybody has the same knowledge base. On the other hand groups as small as two or three appear to benefit greatly from shared outlining and shared drawing tools. Large groups also do very well with shared outlines, but do poorly with shared drawings. It becomes clear that a meeting leader or facilitator must understand not only how to work a GSS tool but what group dynamics it can create.

Culture

Finally, an important attribute that until recently has not received much GSS research attention, concerns the *culture* of the group Most GSS research has focused on American organizations. Yet, research shows that groups from different cultural backgrounds prefer different situations, see e.g. (Hofstede,1980). A great deal of work has yet to be done to discern what benefits of GSS will transfer European, South American, Asian, and African cultures and what special arrangements need to be made to make the application of GSS successful in these environments.

Meeting Environments of the Future

Early GSS research and development focused on supporting teams that were working in the same place at the same time. Recent advances, however, are causing many people to explore the frontier of distributed teamwork - collaboration among people who may be in the next office or may be around the globe. The communication and coordination difficulties posed by geographical separation are much more severe than for face-to-face groups. Present GSS technology serves distributed teams well for on-line activities, but offers little support for the 50% of the time teams need oral communication. New work is under way to integrate video and voice technology with Internet-based GSS in an effort to overcome the loss of face-to-face discussion. A prototype of such an environment is shown in figure 5.

Researchers are also beginning to investigate the use of special-purpose GSS environments to support particular kinds of problem-solving. For example, groups at the University of Arizona and Delft University of Technology have developed GSS tools and methods to support business process re-engineering using the IDEF method (Dean et al., 1994) and object oriented process modeling and simulation (de Vreede, 1995).

Figure 4. A Prototype Distributed Collaborative Environment (Romano et al., 1997).

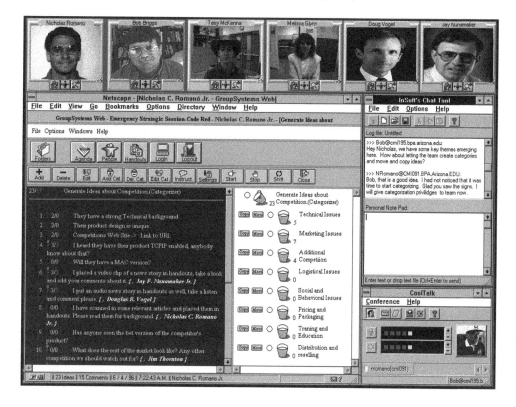

Summary

To summarize, meetings are difficult and expensive, but they are essential for teams that cooperate on complex creative problem-solving tasks. Group Support Systems can be used by teams to significantly reduce their labor costs and to vastly reduce the calendar days required to complete a project.

Technology is no panacea, nor is it a substitute for leadership. However, it can be useful for tasks that require joint cognitive effort to find a creative solution to a complex problem. GSS is not a replacement for oral meetings, but an additional set of methods. When GSS is used conscientiously, experiences from the field and the laboratory environment show that it can produce higher productivity, higher quality output, and highly satisfied groups.

GSS is more than just software for electronic brainstorming and electronic voting. GSS includes not only the software, but also the processes and methods to accompany the use of the tools as well as the environment in which the tools are used. Handled with skill, a GSS can enhance group productivity dramatically. GSS is a new paradigm for collaborative work. The experience of doing business with a GSS is so different from conventional group work that many people have difficulty understanding why they would ever want to use it until they have experienced it personally. Having tried it, many people feel thwarted if they have to return to conventional group work methods. Key benefits many participants identify are the ability to contribute ideas and preference anonymously and in parallel, while having to consciously use a meeting structure that helps the group to stay focused.

GSS tools appear to be changing the reasons groups meet. Instead of just meeting to *plan* their work, the tools allow many groups to actually *do* the work together, in the meeting. This once again stresses the most important critical success factor for electronic meetings: planning ahead. The design of the electronic meeting is critically important. There is a saying among woodworkers, "An apprentice ruins both the wood and the tool." Even so, a GSS must be wielded with intelligence and skill. An unsupported team can wander around for three hours before they figure out they don't know where they are headed. A team using computer-based support can turn a meeting into a train wreck within 10 minutes if team process has not been planned ahead of time. Hence, the key issue is not what the GSS technology *can* do, but rather how a *meeting process can be designed* to maximum advantage, while recognizing and minimizing potential risks.

Chapter Nine

Organizational Use of GSS

How is GSS Used in Different Organizations?

It has been over two decades since Group Support Systems (GSS) emerged on the Information Technology (IT) scene. GSS are defined as socio-technical systems consisting of software, hardware, meeting procedures, facilitation support, and a group of meeting participants engaged in intellectual collaborative work (Eden, 1995; Jessup & Valacich, 1993). GSS are employed to focus and structure group deliberation, while reducing cognitive costs of communication and information access among teams working collaboratively towards a goal (Davison & Briggs, 1994). Early studies in university environments, for example (Gallupe, DeSanctis, & Dickson, 1988), were followed by studies at organizational sites, for example (Grohowski, McGoff, Vogel, Martz, & Nunamaker, 1990). GSS have now been commercialized and are present in an increasing number of domestic and international contexts (Nunamaker, Briggs, Mittleman, Vogel, & Balthazard, 1997).

There is one main question with respect to studies that looked at real organizational groups using GSS: there are comparatively few organizational groups that used GSS in their own environment, i.e. the organization of which they are part. Most studies on real groups report on visits that the group made to facilities outside the organization, most often on the premise of the researchers involved. Exceptions include, e.g., the use of SAMM by the IRS in New York City (DeSanctis, Poole, Lewis, & Desharnais, 1997) and GroupSystems at the US Navy ThirdFleet (Briggs et al., 1998).

An additional challenge has been made with respect to the generalizability of field studies results across corporate and national borders. Comparatively few studies have occurred in international contexts, see Nunamaker et al. (2007) or de Vreede, Jones and Mgaya (1998) for an overview. Those that have occurred have involved use of university facilities, for example (Mejias, Shepherd, Vogel, & Lazaneo, 1997). It would be interesting to investigate the day-to-day use of GSS in organizations headquartered outside the US It is a matter of not only academic curiosity but also of practical relevance to multi-national and international corporations to find out how (or if) results generated in US organizations compare to those generated in international contexts. This knowledge can support investment decisions concerning the implementation of GSS facilities. It can also inform decisions whether or not to put GSS forward as a company-wide 'best practice' to be used locally or across borders by multi-national teams.

In this chapter we present a study (de Vreede, Kolfschoten, & Wien, 2003) that compares and contrasts finding from International Business Machines (IBM) and Boeing Aircraft Corporation in the US with those from Two European companies: Nationale-Nederlanden (NN), the largest insurance firm in the

Netherlands, and European Aeronautic Defense and Space company; Military division, the producer of the Eurofighter. First, we discuss organizational studies on GSS in more detail. Second, we elaborate on our research approach. Third, we discuss the results of our comparative study in which attention is given to aspects of efficiency, effectiveness, and user satisfaction as well as group dynamics. Special emphasis is given to comparison across contexts in field settings and illustrations of return on investment as organizations seek to develop support (if warranted) for embracing GSS on the way to broader distributed use. Finally, we discuss the results and conclude the paper with a summary of the most important findings and implications for further research.

Background

GSS have been studied in a number of fashions, e.g., laboratory experiments, field studies, field experiments, and surveys (Fjermestad & Hiltz, 1998, 2000; de Vreede & Wijk, 1997). There have especially been a relatively large number of laboratory studies (Pervan, 1998; Zigurs, 1993). These studies have most often used student groups without a past or a future. Results have been mixed. Although some studies have reflected positively on the use of GSS, others have not. Over time some attempts have been made to compare results across these lab studies. For example, Gray et al. (1990) noted consistency within groups with similar characteristics but other characteristics and study focus were too varied to draw conclusions. Dennis et al. (1990) found that GSS use improves decision quality and quantity of results. Large groups using GSS appear to benefit more than smaller groups. A comprehensive overview of laboratory studies is given in (Fjermestad & Hiltz, 1998).

Studies of GSS in the field have occurred in two fashions. In the first, researchers have invited organizations to use university facilities, see for example (Applegate, 1991; Dennis, Heminger, Nunamaker, & Vogel, 1990; de Vreede et al., 1998). It is important (and convenient) to do such studies in university contexts where variables can be more systematically explored and sufficient sample sizes be developed under more controlled circumstances. In the second, researchers have studied organizational groups in situ. Only a few examples of such studies exist. For example, Poole et al. 1993 used SAMM developed at the University of Minnesota at Texaco as well as other organizations. Jarvenpaa et al. (1993) used a specially developed prototype at MCC. Five studies used GroupSystems, developed at the University of Arizona:

1. *International Business Machines.* GroupSystems was introduced at IBM in 1987. A series of studies at this site followed that demonstrated that GSS technology could be effectively introduced in

organizational environments (Grohowski, McGoff, Vogel, Martz, & Nunamaker, 1990; Vogel, Nunamaker, Martz, Grohowski, & McGoff, 1990). Based on success at the first facility, IBM installed the technology at six more sites over the following year and similarly expanded their internal facilitation support capabilities (Grohowski et al., 1990; Martz, Vogel, & Nunamaker, 1992; Vogel et al., 1990). IBM continued expanding internally to 24 sites and beyond with the same format of use e.g., pre-planned session agendas with facilitation support throughout the meeting process. The facilitation role has been institutionalized with several generations of facilitators emerging from a wide variety of backgrounds and levels of experience with group and organizational dynamics.

2. *Boeing Aircraft Corporation.* A study was also carried out at Boeing Aircraft Corporation that, encouraged by reports of IBM's success, decided in 1990 to conduct a carefully controlled pilot test of GroupSystems in their organization. Boeing collected data so that a business case could be developed either in favor of, or against the wide-spread use of GSS to support their projects. After 64 sessions, costs were evaluated. The flowtime, or number of calendar days required to produce the deliverables, was reduced by an average of 91%. The man-hour cost savings averaged 71%, or an average of $7,242 per session, for a total savings of $463,488 over the 64 sessions (Post, 1993). This was despite the fact that expense figures included the initial start-up of installing the meeting room technology, training facilitators, and collecting the measurement data.

3. *World Bank.* Another study was carried out more recently at the World Bank headquarters in Washington. In this study, a historical account was given of the acquisition, installation, and early experiences with GroupSystems (Bikson, 1996). The results indicate that after a very successful pilot period in which 102 sessions were organized, the members of the organization accepted the technology as a means of conducting more participative and more effective meetings. As a result of the successful initial adoption of the technology at the organization's headquarters, it has been decided to take the technology to the field as well, see e.g. Jones and Miller (1997).

4. *Nationale-Nederlanden.* A study that, in part, is the focus of this paper was carried out at Nationale-Nederlanden (NN). Part of the ING Group, NN is the largest insurance firm in the Netherlands and one of the market leaders in Europe. NN was introduced to GSS at Delft University of Technology in 1995. Based on early success, NN continued to use GSS and develop its own internal facilitation capabilities (de Vreede, 2000). Following the successful use at NN, other parts of the ING Group have also started to use the technology.

5. *U.S. Navy Commander, Third Fleet.* During a longitudinal field study on board the U.S.S. CORONADO, researchers investigated the acceptance, use, and diffusion of GSS by U.S. Navy staff (Briggs et al., 1998). In the course of the study, the researchers supported various groups in a number of exercises. The study focused on understanding why certain groups of users became self-sustaining over time while others did not. Based on their insights, the researchers state a number of guidelines for establishing an effective GSS facility.

6. *European Aeronautic Defense and Space Company, Military division.* EADS-M is a cooperation of four European companies' in producing the Eurofighter and other military aircrafts. EADS-M was first introduced to GSS by Delft University of Technology in 2001. Based on a successful study on added value of the GSS for the company, a GroupSystems license was acquired and internal facilitators were trained.

Table 1. Overview of Some GSS Field Studies and Their Findings.

(de Vreede et al., 2003).

Source	Context	Findings
Nunamaker et al. 1987 (28)	100 planners in 7 groups from 3 organizations	Decreased idea generation inhibition, anonymity separated status, authority and roles from comments, equal participation opportunity, high participant satisfaction.
Nunamaker et al. 1989 (29)	Various IBM meetings	Higher perceived and measured meeting effectiveness and efficiency, improved meeting outcome quality, high participant satisfaction.
George et al. 1992 (16)	Tucson office of the Indian Health Service	Despite successful GSS introduction, GSS adoption failed: the facility was dismantled after 9 months due to lack of use.
Post 1993 (32)	Various Boeing meetings	Higher perceived and measured meeting effectiveness and efficiency, higher quality of meeting results, high participant satisfaction.
Tyran et al. 1992 (33)	8 strategic management cases in 5 organizations	Higher participation, higher perceived meeting efficiency, more equality of participation, little evaluation apprehension and cross-hierarchical communication support.
Dennis 1994 (5)	10 meetings involving 5 organizations	Higher perceived meeting effectiveness and efficiency, high participant satisfaction.
Emery 1994 (12)	GSS for IS requirement determination	Perceived efficiency improvement without sacrificing effectiveness.
Krcmar et al. 1994 (23)	50 meetings with various organizations	Parallelism perceived to be most useful, divergent perception of usefulness anonymity, perceived correlation between meeting success and task clarity, equal participation, and meeting room comfort.
Bikson 1996 (2)	102 meetings in the World Bank	High participant satisfaction with methods and technology, perception of increased effectiveness and participation.
Herik and Vreede 1997 (19)	2 cases at Ministry of Spatial Planning, Housing and the Environment	High satisfaction with the technology itself, but a neutral evaluation of outcome quality and effectiveness. Positive perception on efficiency and anonymity, but GSS offered too little support for debating and negotiations.
Vreede and Wijk 1997 (37)	9 Nationale-Nederlanden Insurance meetings	Higher perceived and measured meeting effectiveness and efficiency, higher perceived quality of results, high participant satisfaction.

In field studies, researchers have typically assessed the use of GSS to solve real organizational problems. The results from field studies have tended to be more cohesive than those from laboratory experiments (Fjermestad & Hiltz, 1998). In Dennis et al. (1991), a specific comparison of laboratory and field studies noted that differences were not so much a matter of incompatible results as a function of characteristics of the groups, task, and technology. Those laboratory experiments that tended to exhibit characteristics of organization groups tended to generate similar results. Furthermore, the results from GSS field studies predominantly paint a *positive* picture. Some can even be considered as 'success stories', see the illustrative overview presented in Table 1, in which a number of field studies and their findings are summarized. This overview suggests that teams using GSS to support creative problem solving may have more effective and efficient meetings than teams that use manual processes.

Research Approach

In this study, we have set out to compare GSS results from four international organizations that were collected over a time span of 15 years. Results are compared in different contexts and cultures. It explores the differences that might occur as a function of organizational context while being relatively consistent in group- and task characteristics as well as the type of GSS applied.

Setting

In this comparative case study, we use four organizational settings i.e., International Business Machines (IBM), Boeing Aircraft Corporation, Nationale-Nederlanden (NN) and European Aeronautic Defense and Space Company; Military division (EADS-M)

IBM is well known worldwide as a manufacturer of computer hardware and software plus a service provider for those products. The data reported in this study was gathered at an IBM manufacturing plant with approximately 6000 employees located in a rural setting in upstate New York. A room to house the GSS was remodeled according to the design of an operational facility at the University of Arizona. In the room, a U-shaped table was equipped with ten networked microcomputers. An additional microcomputer attached to a large screen projection system was also on the network to enable display of work done at individual workstations or of aggregated information from the total group.

Boeing Aircraft Corporation is mainly known as a designer and manufacturer of airplanes of all sizes, but especially the large ones. With more than 160,000 employees globally, the company has a rich diverse infrastructure, making the mapping of teamwork composition very difficult. This magnitude and vitality makes this organization very suitable for GSS. Encouraged by the success of the research at IBM Boeing initiated a highly controlled test of GroupSystems in their organization in 1990.

NN, is the largest insurance firm in the Netherlands and one of the market leaders in Europe. The firm's products include life, accident, and health insurance as well as financial services. The firm operates in a turbulent market. There are many competitors and their number is increasing, while the market itself is saturated. NN was introduced to GSS at Delft University of Technology in 1995. Positive initial experiences triggered the management to request the researchers from Delft to assess the added value of GSS for their company. For this purpose, over 40 GSS meetings were organized and evaluated. The first two sessions were held at University facilities followed by mobile use at a variety of corporate locations in the Netherlands.

EADS-M is a European cooperation of several European companies with as main project, the development of the Eurofighter aircraft. The study was done at EADS-Military situated at Ottobrunn (Germany). The GSS was situated in a computer classroom for computer education, not very suitable for GSS meetings causing problems in verbal communication. Based on initial experiences with GroupSystems during an internal project, facilitated by Delft, University of Technology, a request for further research on the added value of the GSS for EADS-M was a result. After the pilot project the system was acquired (winter 2001) and facilitation training has taken place (spring 2002).

Research model

The research model for our study illustrated in figure 1 is drawn from prior research (Dennis et al., 1991) and expanded upon in (Nunamaker et al., 1991). This model was used to guide the collection and analysis of data on GSS use in both organizational contexts. This model is useful for the following reasons. First, it is a *descriptive* model and our study is a *descriptive* study. Second, it has been proven useful in many other studies, see e.g. (Herik & de Vreede, 1997; Martz et al., 1992; Nunamaker et al., 1998). Finally, the model enables a way to classify and organize many critical incidents reported in a case study on GSS use (see Figure 1).

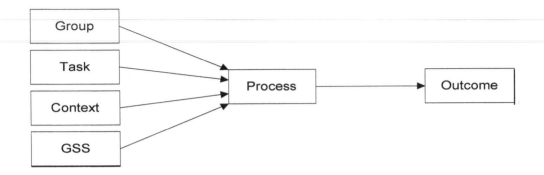

Figure 1. The research model used in the study.

The model addresses issues related to individual, group, project, and organizational levels of analysis that we feel are particularly relevant to GSS design and implementation. The characteristics of the group, task, context, and technology are represented as influencing process which, in turn, influences outcomes.

- Group characteristics data collected include size and the composite of experience, cohesiveness, motivation, and history that constitutes group member attitudes and involvement.

- Task characteristics data include task type, complexity, and task application area.

- Context characteristics data include the organizational environments such as area of business, nationality, and organizational culture.

- Technology characteristics data include GSS hardware, software, and setting configuration.

- Process characteristics data include aspects of the procedures, anonymity, level of participation, facilitation, and interaction of group members during the GSS meetings.

- Group outcomes data include issues such as satisfaction, quality of outcomes, time required to reach resolution, consensus, and decision confidence.

Our method of analysis is based upon multiple sources of data. Questionnaires and post session interviews as well as expert estimation, observation, and system logs all played a role. Specifically, we revisit IBM and Boeing data and compare it to data collected from NN and EADS-M under comparable group, task, and technology characteristics.

Comparison and Contrast

In the previous sections we discussed the organizational context of all four organizations. This section will provide some general information about the task, technology and context at the different organizations in terms of our model in Figure 1. We note a number of comparisons and contrasts that establish the foundation of this study:

- Groups in the IBM and Boeing study had an average size of 8, which compares favorably with NN average group size of 10 and an average size of 7 at EADS-M.

- Task characteristics at IBM and Boeing were best described as "problem solving" and covered a wide range of application areas similar to those addressed by NN. Differently, at EADS-M the GSS was mostly used for kick-off meetings exploring goals and boundaries of new projects. Task structure and size varied considerably across the 4 organizations.

- Technology in all four cases was GroupSystems developed at the University of Arizona and commercialized by GroupSystems.com (formerly known as Ventana Corporation). Although operating systems have changed from DOS to Windows, tool characteristics and functionality remain comparable. The studies conducted at IBM and Boeing used DOS-based GroupSystems while NN and EADS-M used Windows-based GroupSystems.

- The participants at all four sites were sufficiently computer literate to participate meaningfully. Their training on the use of the GSS never took more than 15 to 20 minutes. No participant abandoned the technology during the sessions. No participant expressed concerns that they could not participate meaningfully in the meeting.

Results

Data for this comparative study were collected from 441 participants in 55 groups at IBM, 654 participants in 64 groups at Boeing, 414 participants in 39 groups at NN and 74 participants in 10 groups at EADS-M. Below we present the results with respect to process and technology, efficiency, effectiveness, user satisfaction, and cost benefit respectively. Detailed accounts of the IBM studies can be found in (Grohowski et al, 1990; Martz et al., 1992; Nunamaker et al., 1989; Vogel et al., 1990); the Boeing study can be found in (Post, 1993); the NN study can be found in (de Vreede, 2000); and the

EADS-M data are reported in this paper. All participants' perceptions were on a 5 point scale, 5 being the most positive.

Process and Technology

Findings on interaction, participation, anonymity and parallel working were only available for IBM, NN and EADS-M. Participants in the organizations agreed on various process and technology aspects. IBM participants felt that in a manual group setting it would be extremely difficult to get the same amount of *interaction* as in a GSS meeting. NN participants rated the extent to which GSS encourage interaction 3.8 while EADS-M participants rated it 3.9. The meetings logs of the sessions at IBM and feedback from participants suggested that very high levels of *participation* were achieved, and, in addition, GSS were thought to equalize participation. The participants in NN and EADS-M sessions rated the extent to which GSS encourage participation 4.0 and 4.1 respectively. However, some participants at NN also remarked that although the process gave everyone an equal chance to contribute, the electronic discussions were sometimes somewhat impersonal and therefore they did not feel very motivated to participate. This effect was also observed at EADS-M, aggravated by the 'classroom setting' in which some sessions took place.

Members from both organizations were very positive about the *anonymity* feature of GSS. NN and EADS-M participants rated the functionality of anonymous communication 4.3 and 4.7 respectively, and the extent to which they liked working anonymously 4.2 and 4.1 respectively At all three organizations some sessions would not have been possible without anonymity. At IBM and EADS-M people felt less apprehensive to contribute ideas and discuss them openly. Anonymity was considered to be instrumental to achieve a process that lacked intimidation. At NN and EADS-M anonymity was thought to be especially valuable when sensitive subjects were discussed. At NN and EADS-M some participants felt taken seriously for the first time. At EADS-M anonymity was not always used, and once was considered a barrier because the participants discussed critical aspects and all wanted to know each other's contributions to have a profound discussion about these aspects. The high rate for the functionality of anonymity at EADS-M was believed to be due to the importance of hierarchy in the organization.

The organizations subscribed to the notion that *parallel* input of ideas and votes can boost productivity. Both at NN and EADS-M participants remarked that notwithstanding its advantages, parallel communication comes with the risk of overloading the participants with information. The NN participants rated the extent to which they liked working in parallel, EADS-M 4.7.

Efficiency

Efficiency was expressed by the participants in terms of perceptions as well as comparison with historical sessions. Some comparative results are presented in Table 2. At IBM, participants rated at 3.9 that the session is efficient, at Boeing and NN participants rated 4.0 and EADS-M rated it 4.3. Also, NN participants perceived that "available time was used well" at 4.1 and EADS-M rated it 4.2. In addition, NN and EADS-M participants scored on "this GSS meeting is more productive than a manual meeting".

Additional data was gathered from session leaders. Prior to GSS use, and without knowledge of automated support capabilities, group leaders were required to recommend and document a feasible project schedule for objective accomplishment based on experience with previous similar projects. After completion of the project, expectations before use of the tools was compared with what actually occurred. Person hours were saved in the cases recorded, with an average per session saving of 55.5% at IBM, 71% at Boeing ,53.0% at NN and 49.7% at EADS-M. The same procedure was followed for calendar time savings. At NN, 57.7 % savings was recorded, while at IBM significantly higher levels at 92 % and 89 % percent for two series of sessions were estimated. Also Boeing was higher, at 91%. On the contrary EADS-M was significantly lower, 33.3%. We belief that low calendar saving time is due to the fact that meetings were mostly kick-off meetings and exact time savings were hard to estimate by initiators because there were no similar projects to compare with.

Table 2. Summary of results on efficiency, effectiveness, and user satisfaction.
(de Vreede et al., 2003)

Aspect	IBM	Boeing	NN	EADS-M
Efficiency				
Session is efficient	3.9	4.0	4.0	4.3
Person hours savings	55.5 %	71.0%	53.0 %	49.7%
Calendar time savings	92 % / 89 %[1]	91.0%	57.7 %	33.3%
Effectiveness				
GSS more effective than manual	4.2	n.a.	4.0	4.1
GSS helps to achieve goals	4.1	4.0	3.9	4.0
Initiator's evaluation of outcome quality	4.4	4.1	3.9	4.3
User satisfaction				
Satisfaction with GSS process	4.1	n.a.	4.1	4.3
Willingness to use GSS in similar projects/activities	4.2[2]	4.4	4.2	4.5

[1] based on 11 and 59 sessions respectively. [2] for brainstorming activities

Effectiveness

Effectiveness was comprised of two main components: extent of goal achievement and quality of outcome. It appears that IBM participants were slightly more positive on effectiveness aspects than NN, EADS-M and Boeing participants, see table 2. At IBM, participants rated at 4.2 that the GSS exercise was more effective than a manual procedure. At Boeing these date were not available, at NN it was rated 4.0 and at EADS-M and 4.1. Also, GSS were considered to be instrumental in helping the group to achieve its goals. This was rated 4.1 for IBM, 4.0 for Boeing, 3.9 for NN and 4.0 for EADS-M. The session initiators' perspective on the quality of the outcomes of the session were most positive at IBM as well, 4.4 compared to 4.1 at Boeing, 3.9 at NN and 4.3 at EADS-M. Yet, overall patterns of perceptions on effectiveness were very similar.

User satisfaction

All sites scored high on user satisfaction aspects. Both at IBM and NN, user satisfaction with the process was rated at 4.1. At Boeing no data were recorded on this aspect, at EADS-M satisfaction with the process was rated 4.3. Participants at NN and EADS-M noted at 3.7 and 3.9 respectively that the "results met expectations". "GSS was useful for today's activities" was rated 4.1 at NN and 4.0 at EADS-M . Asking whether they would be willing to use GSS in similar projects the participants at both IBM and NN responded 4.2. Boeing rated 4.4 and EADS-M 4.5.

Most data on user satisfaction, however, came from follow-up interviews. Participants at IBM noted numerous benefits over traditional meetings including enhanced group synergism, reduction in participant apprehension, openness of the process, and lack of intimidation. NN participants stated that they liked the immediate availability of meeting minutes, the fairness of the process. They also felt the technology and the way it was applied helped them to better achieve consensus on a number of issues. Meeting initiators stressed that they most appreciated the comparatively higher quality of meeting results. Higher meeting efficiency was less important to them. Yet, at EADS-M efficiency was evaluated as a very important aspect. In some of the projects meeting the deadlines was more important than quality. The GSS enabled them to achieve both quality and the deadline. The immediate availability of meeting minutes was also recognized at EADS-M as very positive.

Cost / Benefit

A key element of acceptance the different companies was the relation between the costs and benefits of a GSS facility. All organizations were especially interested in ascertaining whether GSS could provide a measure of savings in people hours that would offset the cost of specially developed facilities and associated support necessary to sustain a long-term program of use.

Based on 64 cases at IBM with 490 participants, $157,315 (1987) of savings was attained, more than enough to recover full annual support costs. The 64 cases were essentially the equivalent of 32 days of facility use, 15% of those available for use over the course of a year. At Boeing, $432,260 (1993)was saved in 64 sessions with 654 participants in total resulting in a satisfying return of investment and a well-founded decision to acquire the system. At NN, $143,000 (2001) of annual savings were estimated if 104 sessions were organized. The break-even point for the facility at NN, including personnel, hardware, and software, would be after three years. Annual support costs would be covered by 35 days of facility use. At EADS-M savings of $40,000 (2002) for 10 sessions, more than enough to cover the pilot phase expenses. The annual number of full day sessions to break even over a 3 year period is 28 at EADS-M.

Discussion

The number of NN and EADS-M sessions were fewer in number compared to IBM and Boeing. Further, IBM and Boeing tended to use its own facilitators, who were initially trained by the University of Arizona, and quickly developed a stylized form of moderation. This is in contrast with NN and EADS-M which relied solely on Delft University of Technology facilitators who were present during all sessions (although since the sessions reported in the study were held, at both sites internal facilitators have been trained who applied GroupSystems in real sessions).

There are numerous salient issues that arise from the comparison between the four sites. Overall, the results from the studies are strikingly similar. This is particularly interesting given the different nature of the organizations and their employees:

- The studies were conducted in a time span of 16 years. In time the pervasiveness (or lack thereof) of computer technology in general and GSS in particular has changed dramatically.

- All organizations are very different - in terms of basic business interests in general and vested interest in computers in particular.

- All organizations recognized the usefulness of GSS features such as anonymity and parallel communication in spite of significant differences in group-makeup and experience in working together.

- Technology diffusion has continued at IBM, Boeing and NN as they took more responsibility for session initiation and facilitation as time progressed. At EADS-M implementation of the GSS is still in progress.

There were, however, differences in the results that may to some extent be attributed to characteristics of the organizations and their people:

- At the US companies and EADS-M, it was stated that timesaving absolutely represented the biggest advantage of the system. At NN, however, time savings were not considered most important. Many participants, including session initiators felt that the biggest advantage was the perceived higher quality of meeting outcomes. This may also be an explanation for NN initiators' more critical evaluation of outcome quality than the initiators at other companies. At NN, employees tended to put less emphasis on the importance of facilitation in contrast to IBM, Boeing and EADS-M where employees relied heavily on facilitation before, during, and after sessions. To some extent, this explains the desire, from the beginning, to quickly develop own personnel as facilitators and recognize it as a critical success factor.

- At IBM, a stylized pattern of GSS use quickly emerged i.e., brainstorming, organizing, and vote that varied little as a function of task characteristics. At NN and EADS-M, session agendas were more varied as group leaders and facilitators sought to achieve a fit to difference challenges. The main explanation for this may be the difference between in-house facilitators who are full-time organizational employees (IBM) and those who are brought in more in a consultative role, especially when they are academics (NN and EADS-M). Academics may be more likely to explore and try different things. Corporate employee facilitators may be less likely to explore and less likely to take risks. Consultants can walk away from a failure, employees have to live with it. This is likely to invoke different facilitator behavior with different objectives – not right or wrong but definitely different.

- At IBM, norms of behavior were made very explicit, including an opening screen of "don'ts," e.g., do not criticize during brainstorming. At NN and EADS-M, behavior was more relaxed and varied with no fixed modes of required or preferred behavior.

Neither of the IBM, NN and EADS-M studies addresses longer-term issues of innovation diffusion and organizational institutionalization of GSS such as reported in (Bikson, 1996) and Briggs et al., 1998). It remains to be seen how examples as reported here affect organizations as a whole. For example, yet to be studied is the impact on the organization of GSS in terms of structuring to meet future needs. At Boeing, the total working process was adjusted to the GSS, leading to a higher level of efficiency but detailed information about the effect on the organization as a whole are not available.

Summary

There has been a paucity of studies of organizations using GSS in situ, especially in international contexts. Reasons for this are many. It is often difficult to develop trust to the extent that organizations will try new technology. New technology requires attention and expense that often exceed immediate expectations of return. Unlike universities, organizations by nature are not as interested in exploring concepts and have removing uncertainty as their primary focus. Further, it is often difficult to systematically collect data. Organizations are rarely interested in spending time filling out questionnaires or having their data presented in public.

In this paper, we have revisited data from IBM and Boeing and compared it to data collected from NN and EADS-M. Overall, the results are more striking in their similarities than differences. In all studies, GSS provided consistent added value. This is especially interesting given the independent nature of the studies. Much remains to be done, however. Ultimately, it is important to use a variety of approaches to explore GSS application and implications as the technology diffuses in global organizational contexts. The experience from all four studies and this comparative study lead us the following areas of future research:

1. There is a need for studying the application of GSS that goes beyond one or a few sessions. Relatively little is known about the way in which groups can use GSS consistently in lengthy projects. Moreover, there is a need to study organizations were GSS have or are about to become an embedded part of the organization's primary processes, such as software companies and educational institutions. Although all organizations have adopted a GSS, more research has to be done about how to use the GSS on a regular basis as a part of standard processes instead of using it as an ad hoc tool for unique sessions or problems.

2. All companies have multiple locations, all are international, therefore research on distributed sessions would be interesting and useful. GroupSystems.com has developed an online version of

GroupSystems, which offers the same functionality as the meeting room version. The research model and focus of the studies presented in this paper could function as a blueprint for research into distributed collaboration so that differences in participant perceptions between the two collaboration modi can be illuminated and investigated.

3. Finally, it would be advisable to develop a framework for studying the organizational application of GSS so that the results from various studies become comparable. Such a framework would have to look at various aspects of GSS use in organizations, such as group behavior, performance, cost/benefit, and adoption of technology over time.

Chapter Ten

Collaboration Engineering

Facilitators can be a costly option for an organization, and so, many groups that could benefit from their services do not have access to them. Unfortunately, it can be challenging for an organization to retain its facilitators because, as articulate, problem-solving people-oriented employees who are comfortable with technology, they are often either promoted to new positions or they leave the organization to establish consulting practices (Agres et al., 2005).

Over the past decade, researchers have, therefore, been developing, applying, and evaluating ways to design productive, task-specific work practices that practitioners, who are not professional facilitators, can successfully execute for themselves (de Vreede, Briggs, & Massey, 2009). This research has addressed collaboration from a holistic perspective: focusing simultaneously on the details of a work practice, the configuration and packaging of required technology and on documentation of the guidance that practitioners must give a group to move it through useful patterns of collaboration toward its goals. This stream of research has come to be called *Collaboration Engineering*.

Collaboration Engineering concerns the design and deployment of collaboration processes for recurring high-value collaborative tasks. In Collaboration Engineering, a *collaboration engineer* designs a reusable and predictable collaboration process for a recurring task including technological support, and transfers the design to *practitioners* to execute for themselves without the ongoing intervention of *group process professionals*, i.e. facilitators. These practitioners are domain experts, but are not necessarily experts in designing new collaboration processes for themselves or others. They execute the designed collaboration process as part of their regular work.

The field of Collaboration Engineering is the focus of this chapter. The Collaboration Engineering field is at the crossroads of many disciplines, among them information systems, computer science, systems engineering, organization science, organizational behavior, education, communication, and social, cognitive, and organizational and industrial psychology (de Vreede, Briggs, & Massey, 2009). Collaboration Engineering researchers often combine insights from these disciplines to find better ways to design a collaborative work process that stimulates self-sustained use by a growing number of practitioners. The need to combine the insights from these various disciplines makes Collaboration Engineering a fertile research domain.

Collaboration Engineering Domain

Collaboration Engineering focuses on *mission-critical* collaborative tasks. A mission-critical task is one which creates substantial value, or which reduces the risk of loss of substantial value for organizational stakeholders. Collaboration Engineering further focuses on processes for mission-critical tasks that are *recurring* and must be executed *frequently*. Examples of frequently recurring collaboration processes can be found in various sectors, for instance financial services, government/defense, and software development:

- Financial services:
- Collaborative enterprise risk assessment
- Collaborative service product development
- Collaborative Sarbanes-Oxley assessments
- Marketing focus groups
- Government/Defense:
- Collaborative crisis response
- Collaborative situational awareness
- Collaborative course of action analysis
- Collaborative document creation and review
- Software development:
- Collaborative requirements negotiation & specification
- Collaborative usability testing
- Collaborative requirements inspections
- Collaborative code inspections

Collaboration Engineering research focuses on frequently-recurring processes rather than ad-hoc processes based on the logic of the Technology Transition Model (TTM) (Briggs et al. 2003) and its successor, the Value Frequency Model (VFM) (Briggs and Murphy in press). Both TTM and VFM predict that individuals are most likely to accept and adopt a change of technology or work practice that brings them substantial value on frequent basis. If improvements are realized for a repeated process, then the organization derives benefit from the improvement again and again. If the focus were on ad-hoc processes, then the value of each process improvement would be obtained only once. In addition, in the case of repeatable processes, practitioners of the process can attain results similar to those of professional facilitators without having to master the complete suite of facilitation skills. They need only learn the small sub-set of techniques necessary to conduct their own work practices.

Various field studies have reported successful implementations of processes designed by collaboration engineers. In these situations, the deployed collaboration processes are conducted by self-sustaining practitioners. (Example 1 presents a summary of one of these cases). A sample of these studies includes the following:

- **ING Group**, a financial services firm, conducts collaborative Risk & Control Self Assessments processes in all of its branches across the world. This case is described in more detail in textbox 1.

- The **U.S. Army's Advanced Research Lab** uses a repeatable collaborative approach to mission analysis (Harder and Higley 2004; Harder et al. 2005).

- The **European Aeronautic Defense and Space company (EADS)** deployed a repeatable process for Manufacturing Project Knowledge Elicitation (Graaff et al. 2005).

- The **Rotterdam Port Authority in the Netherlands** has used Collaboration Engineering techniques to support crisis response training and operational execution (Appelman and Driel 2005).

- A process for collaborative usability testing was successfully employed for the development of a governmental health emergency management system (Fruhling and Vreede 2005).

- A telecom company used a repeatable collaboration process to define and explore new mobile services (Bragge et al. 2005).

- Dozens of groups engaged in effective software requirements negotiations using the EasyWinWin process (Boehm et al. 2001; Grünbacher et al. 2005).

Collaboration Engineering Foundations

A central foundation for Collaboration Engineering is the use of design patterns to support the design and transition of collaborative work practices. As explained in Chapter Two, design patterns and pattern languages can serve several key purposes in collaborative problem solving (Alexander, 1979). First, they provide a convenient common language for communication. They allow designers that know the pattern language to name and share complex concepts without having to explain them over and over again in detail. Second, individual design patterns can be combined to design larger systems. Furthermore, patterns support teaching, capturing, and sharing expert design knowledge.

Also as explained in Chapter Two, the design patterns used in Collaboration Engineering are called thinkLets (de Vreede et al., 2006). A thinkLet is a named, scripted technique for predictably and repeatedly invoking known effects among people working together toward a goal. ThinkLets researchers seek to distill each thinkLet to the smallest unit of intellectual capital necessary to predictably and invoke a desired effect. ThinkLets are reusable, transferable facilitation techniques that can be used to move a group through a process toward its agreed goal (Briggs et al., 2003). They enable rapid development of sophisticated, coherent, multi-layered collaboration processes that can improve the productivity and quality of work life for teams (de Vreede et al. 2006).The example in figure 1 depicts both sides of the FastFocus thinkLet cue card. FastFocus is a facilitation technique for moving a group from having many ideas to a focus on fewer that they deem worthy of more attention.

Figure 1. Cue card for the FastFocus ThinkLet. Words enclosed in angle brackets (<>) are parameters that are replaced with task-specific terms when the thinkLet is instantiated in a collaboration process design (de Vreede et al., 2009).

FastFocus (Reduce, Clarify)

- ## Choose this thinkLet...
  - To quickly extract a clean, non-redundant list from a brainstorm activity
  - When agreement on the meaning of the resulting list is important
- ## Do not choose this thinkLet...
  - To reach consensus on the merits of ideas. Consider the StrawPoll thinkLet instead.
- ## Setup
  - Distribute all brainstorming ideas across multiple pages – at least one page per participant. Give each participant a page of ideas.
  - Create a place where you can create a publicly viewable list of the key ideas they extract from their brainstorming activity

- ## Script
  - Say this:

    "Read through the brainstorming ideas in the page in front of you and look for <important> <ideas>"

    "I will call on each of you in turn. <Person name>, what is the most <important> <idea> on the page in front of you that is not yet on the list?"
  - Do this:

    Write each new idea on the public list
  - Say this if someone proposes an idea that may already be on the list :
    - "Is that idea the same or different from <idea X> on the list?"
  - Do This:
    - When all participants have had a turn, tell everybody to swap pages; start a second round
    - For the third round, ask the whole group if anyone has an <important> <Idea> that is not yet on the list
    - Repeat until no one wants to add anything new to the list

Patterns and pattern based design have found their way into the software engineering, (Gamma et al., 1995), workflow management (Aalst et al., 2003), and project management (Khazanchi & Zigurs, 2006). For example, Lukosch and Schümmer (2004) propose a pattern language for the development of collaborative software.

In Collaboration Engineering, thinkLets are used as building blocks for team process designs in many domains where collaboration is required (de Vreede & Briggs, 2005). Each time a thinkLet is instantiated in a design, its parameters may differ, but nonetheless predictable group dynamics will emerge. For example, Figure 2 depicts a process model of a collaborative risk identification process consisting of a sequence four thinkLets. This four-thinkLet process is a segment of a larger design that has been adopted by ING Group as described in Figure 2.

Figure 2. A thinkLet Sequence for Identifying Risk – used by ING
(de Vreede et al., 2009)

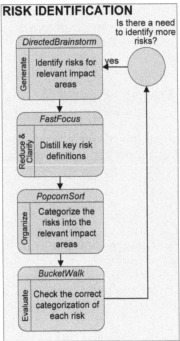

Collaboration Engineering Approach

As an approach, Collaboration Engineering consists of a *design phase*, where the repeatable collaboration processes is designed and piloted, and a *deployment phase*, where the new collaboration process is introduced into the organization and practitioners are trained. A high level overview of the two phases is given in Figure 3.

Figure 3. Overview of the Collaboration Engineering Approach (de Vreede et al., 2009).

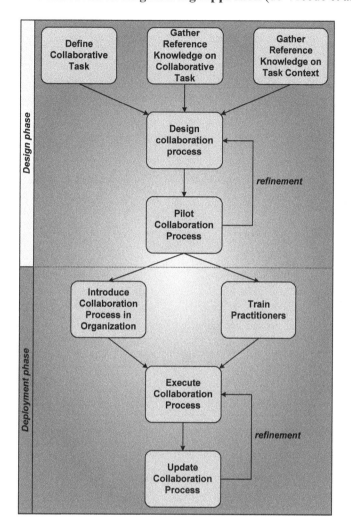

The design phase starts with the identification and definition of a recurring collaborative task that can benefit from a Collaboration Engineering design effort. A collaboration engineer also identifies best practices for this task. These practices are often found in organizational standards, industry standards, or reference literature. In addition, the collaboration engineer has to gather knowledge on the context in which the collaboration process will be executed. This involves, for example, determining relevant characteristics of the groups executing the process, their stakes involved in the process outcomes, and the required task relevant competencies of the practitioners that will guide the process execution.

Next, the collaboration engineer uses these insights to create a first version of the collaboration process design (Kolfschoten &Vreede, in press). In this design effort, the collaborative task is decomposed into a logical sequence of activities that require a pattern of collaboration to be executed by a group. These patterns of collaboration can be created using the collaboration process design patterns, i.e.

thinkLets. In other words, the decomposition provides a basis for matching available thinkLets to the constituent activities of the collaborative task, see Figure 4.

Figure 4. Decomposition of a Collaborative Task into a Sequence of Collaboration Process Design Patterns, i.e. thinkLets (de Vreede et al., 2009).

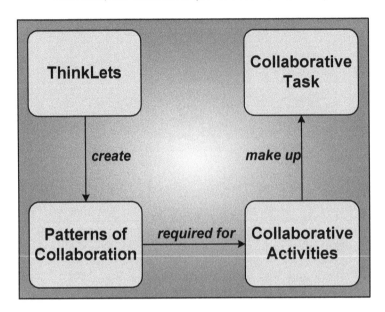

Once the first version of the collaboration process design is completed, it can be validated and executed during one or more pilots. The results of these pilots can lead to refinements to the process. If the pilot results are satisfactory, the collaboration process can be implemented in the organization, starting the deployment phase of the Collaboration Engineering approach.

In the deployment phase, the collaboration process is introduced into the organization. This involves, for example, briefing the relevant stakeholders that will be involved in the process and defining a program of incentives for executing the process according to the new standard. Also practitioners have to be trained to become effective group leaders for the recurring collaboration process. Field research to date has shown that the best results are achieved by combining different training methods, including lectures (for example on patterns of collaboration, thinkLets, and the role of the practitioner), an exercise for the practitioners to construct the activity flow of the collaboration process themselves, simulation and coaching to practice each step of the process in the context of a case situation, and providing execution support in the form of thinkLet cue cards and a complete process overview (Kolfschoten et al., in press). Further feedback and experiences with the collaboration process in practice may result in adaptations and improvement. In larger projects, as in the case of ING Group, communities of practice can be formed among the practitioners to exchange experiences and improve or adapt the process to changes in the organization (Chakrapani, 2005).

Although the design and deployment activities are described and depicted above in a seemingly linear fashion, it should be noted that in reality they are not linear in nature. Depending on the context, the Collaboration Engineering approach requires and allows for iteration and incrementation. Certain design activities are carried out in parallel and on different levels of abstraction. For example, an exploration of existing best practices and designing a process in terms of steps and patterns of collaboration can occur simultaneously. Also, during the piloting of the collaboration process, the collaboration engineer may continuously evaluate the design results so far together with an organizational counterpart and make changes accordingly. In other words, the Collaboration Engineering design approach is not meant to be a cookbook. Rather, it should be seen as a set of design steps. Experience shows that the order in which these design steps are executed depends on the type, complexity, and scope of the collaboration task, and the existing amount of insight in the organization's collaborative task.

Collaboration Engineering Modeling Techniques

An important aspect of designing and deploying repeatable collaboration processes concerns capturing the design artifacts in a useful format. To this end, Collaboration Engineering researchers have developed various techniques to model and document repeatable collaboration processes. Models of a collaboration process should be expressive, comprehensive, unambiguous, and intuitive. Models not only serve as a vehicle of communication among designers, but are also used to present designs to the organization and to support the training of practitioners that will execute the collaboration process. Below we present three modeling conventions that have been developed and widely used over the past few years: the thinkLet documentation format, the Facilitation Process Model and the Agenda Design Format.

ThinkLet Documentation Format. A thinkLet has to capture all information required to create a pattern of collaboration in a predictable, transferable way. To provide consistency and comparability, each thinkLet has to be codified using the same documentation template. As previously described in the chapter on thinkLets, this template consists of three components: the identification, the script, and selection guidance (see Chapter Four for more details and examples).

Facilitation Process Model. A Facilitation Process Model (FPM) is used to display the flow and logical interdependencies between the activities in a collaboration process. An FPM focuses attention on the logic of the flow of the process from activity to activity. An FPM uses three symbols (see Figure 5) to model the flow of a process. Each *activity* in a process is represented by a rectangle with rounded corners that has been divided into five fields. The left upper field indicates the sequence number of the activity. The largest field contains a descriptive name for the activity that conveys what the team is supposed to do. The field on the left names the primary pattern of collaboration to be created during the activity. The thinkLet name to be used for this purpose appears across the top. The upper right corner displays the time required to complete the activity. Each *decision* that may affect the process flow is represented by a circle. Underneath each decision the decision criteria are indicated. Finally, each *flow direction* is represented by an arrow. Underneath or next to the arrow the results from a previous activity can be described. These also represent the input for the next activity. Figure 6 depicts a complete FPM for the example in Figure 1.

Figure 5. Elements of a Facilitation Process Model (de Vreede et al., 2009).

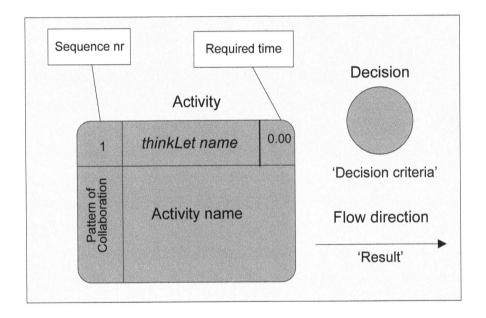

Figure 6. Example of a Facilitation Process Model (de Vreede et al., 2009).

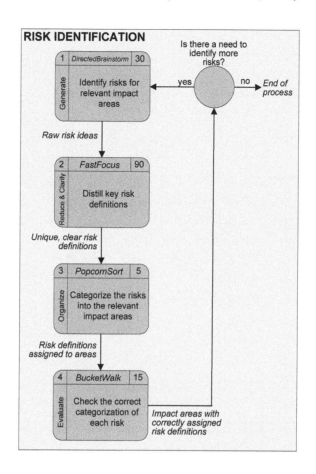

Agenda Design Format. To execute a collaboration process design in practice, more information needs to be recorded than the FPM can provide. The Agenda Design Format (ADF) specifies all relevant information for each activity in the process. This information consists of the name of each activity, the specific questions or assignments that will be provided to the group, the deliverables that have to be created in the activity, the thinkLet to be used with the associated pattern of collaboration and tool on which the thinkLet is to be implemented, and finally the starting time of each activity. Table 1 shows the ADF for the risk identification example in Figures 1 and 5, using the GSS GroupSystems as a tool platform.

Table 1. Example of the agenda format of a collaboration process design (de Vreede et al., 2009)

	Activity	Question/Assignment	Deliverable	ThinkLet (Pattern) Tool	Time
	Introduction to workshop	Introduce goal and deliverable. Goal: Identify key risks for relevant impact areas. Deliverable: A list of clear, unique risk definitions per impact area	Commitment to the goal, understanding GSS, knowing each other	None	9.00
1	Identify risks for relevant impact areas	What are the key risks for the following impact areas: front office, back office, IT, product development, management?	Broad collection of raw risk ideas for various impact areas	DirectedBrainstorm (Generate) EBS	9.20
2	Distill key risk definitions	Please identify and reformulate the most important risk on your sheet	List of unique and clearly defined risks	FastFocus (Reduce & Clarify) EBS and Categorizer	9.50
3	Categorize risks into relevant impact areas	Please place each risk definition into the impact area that is responsible to manage it.	Initial distribution of risks over responsible impact areas	PopcornSort (Organize) Categorizer	11.20
4	Check correct categorization of each risk	Please check for each impact area whether all risks in there have been properly assigned.	Agreed on assignment of risks over responsible impact areas	BucketWalk (Evaluate) Categorizer	11.25
	Decide on whether to identify more risks	If there are sufficient risks defined for each area, then conclude workshop, else go back to step 1 for impact area(s)concerned	Decision on whether to identify more risks	None	11.50

Collaboration Engineering Research Agenda

Since the start of Collaboration Engineering research in 2001, over a 100 scholarly works have been published by researchers across the world. Many field applications have taken place. Research efforts have focused on various theories underlying Collaboration Engineering and on the development of metric and instruments to assess the quality of Collaboration Engineering interventions and designs (see Figure 7). Studies have employed a variety of research strategies, including field studies like case studies and action research, laboratory experiments, and prototype development. Studies have taken place in

© The Center for Collaboration Science

different physical environments (e.g. face to face or virtual collaboration) and in different or mixed social or cultural settings.

Figure 7. Overview of the Collaboration Engineering research area (de Vreede, 2009).

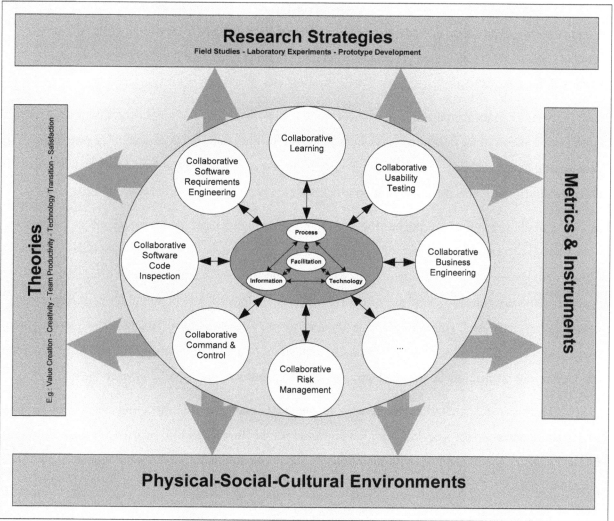

Although many encouraging results have been reported, many academic and practical challenges and opportunities lie ahead to further develop the Collaboration Engineering research area in terms of it foundations, its design and deployment approach, and its modeling techniques. Below is a number of these research challenges and opportunities.

Foundations. There is a plethora of research opportunities with respect to the foundations of Collaboration Engineering. On the group level, decades of research have yielded many insights into group behavior in the context of a particular group task (e.g., Dennis 2001; Fjermestad & Hiltz, 1999). The literature shows that much of this research has focused on brainstorming. Deeper theoretical understanding of other collaborative activities is greatly needed. In particular, future research should focus on the theoretical foundations of that reduce, clarify, evaluate, organize, and build consensus patterns of collaboration.

On the organizational level, there is a need for further fundamental research on how groups and organizations accept, adopt, and adapt repeatable collaboration processes. How do groups embrace a standard repeatable collaboration process over time? How do they change it themselves over time to better suit their needs?

Another fundamental challenge concerns the quality assessment of a collaboration process design. How can we measure the design of a collaboration process either before it is executed (i.e. the 'paper' design) or during execution? And, is it possible to create a quality assessment framework that is independent from the specific collaboration process that is being assessed or its context?

Collaboration Engineering has focused mainly on designing and deploying 'fixed' collaboration process design: a standard sequence of collaborative activities modeled with collaboration design patterns (thinkLets). However, there are situations in which a single standard sequence cannot offer adequate support. These are situations were more creative, ad hoc solutions have to be found for recurring collaborative challenges. Think for example about crisis response situations. This begs the question whether it would be possible to define a standard repository of a limited number of thinkLets that a group can then use by themselves to create adaptive process sequences as and when they need them.

More research is also required to explore whether Collaboration Engineering can only be applied to design organization specific collaboration processes, or whether it can also be used to design processes that are industry specific, for example an industry standard on collaborative software engineering project post-mortems.

Finally, a key issue for collaboration engineers concerns the cultural context in which the repeatable collaboration process has to be executed. To what extent is Collaboration Engineering culturally bound? To what extent can thinkLets-based processes be applied in different cultures? How is the role of a practitioner perceived in different cultures? ING Group's experiences show that their standard collaborative risk assessment process was successfully accepted and applied in over 30 countries in North and South America, Europe, Asia, and Australia. However, some Asian cultures showed a high reluctance and very low diffusion rates.

Design and Deployment Approach. To date, most Collaboration Engineering studies have focused on face-to-face settings. As virtual team work and virtual work environments are becoming a more dominant setting in which (inter)-organizational work is done, the applicability of Collaboration Engineering concepts to virtual collaboration has to be explored. This includes seeking out and capturing effective design patterns and deriving design guidelines for virtual collaboration processes.

Another research opportunity concerns the characteristics of the individuals that fulfill the practitioner's role. Practitioners are domain experts but not collaboration experts. Not everyone that has a deep understanding of an application domain is necessarily suited to be an effective group leader for repeatable processes in this domain. It could increase the likelihood that practitioners become effective group leaders if we have a deeper understanding of the personality characteristics that are shared among successful facilitators. Thus, the question to ask is whether people with a natural flair for guiding group work share similar personalities? If so, then these personality characteristics could be used as a way to identify and select candidate practitioners within an organization.

Modeling Techniques. The current Collaboration Engineering modeling techniques that are used to document collaboration process designs were developed through experiences in a large number of field studies. A next phase in the development of these techniques should focus on strengthening their theoretical basis in two ways. First, the different models should be unified by developing a meta-model that specifies all relevant elements in a collaboration process design and the interdependencies between these elements. Based on that unified meta-model, different aspect models could be formally defined. Each aspect model could highlight a particular perspective on the collaboration process design, like the FPM is currently highlighting the flow of the process logic and the ADF focuses on the specific instructions given to the group and the desired deliverables in each activity in the process.

Second, based on a unified meta-model, a formal model syntax of each of the modeling techniques could be derived. Such a syntax would provide a basis to ensure that models adhere to a minimum quality standard. They could also provide a starting point to develop guidelines or model checks to (automatically) assess the quality of collaboration process models.

Tool Support. There are various opportunities to develop Computer Assisted Collaboration Engineering (CACE) tools. For example, tools can be developed to support design activities. Examples of tool support in this area include, but are not limited to providing guidance in the choice of thinkLets to match process activities, drawing Facilitation Process Models, or providing automatic design guidance during the construction of an Agenda Design Format.

Tools can also be developed to support the documentation of thinkLets. As thinkLets are used by various collaboration engineers and many experiences are gathered in the field, updates to these thinkLets are inevitable. To enable consistency and accuracy in the formal definition of each thinkLet according to the template presented in section 5 a thinkLet content management tool would be useful.

A final area where tool support can advance the Collaboration Engineering area concerns the actual execution of collaboration process designs. Currently collaboration process design have to be implemented on general collaboration software platforms, such as commercial GSS. As these platforms offer many more functionalities or configurations than are needed in any particular recurring collaboration process, they are very complex to operate for practitioners. To overcome this challenge, a design studio could be developed that allows a collaboration engineer not only to capture the logic of collaboration process but also the guidance that the practitioner needs to execute it. The studio would then instantiate the design including guidance as a stand-alone application that the practitioner and his or her group can run any time the process needs to be executed. Such a studio would make collaboration technologies more accessible and useable than general purpose GSS suites.

Summary

Collaboration is a critical phenomenon in organizational life. Collaboration is necessary yet difficult to do well. The field of IS has devoted many efforts to understanding how groups can and will use technologies to improve the productivity of their collaborative work. Over the past decade, the field of Collaboration Engineering has emerged as a focal point for research on designing and deploying collaboration processes that are recurring in nature and that are executed by practitioners in organizations rather than collaboration professionals.

In this chapter we have highlighted the foundations of the Collaboration Engineering field, given an overview of the design and deployment activities and modeling techniques. The insights presented in this paper represent the results of many studies and field applications that have been made possible through the efforts of an international community of researchers. We hope that past results and future opportunities will inspire many more to become active in this exciting field of research.

Chapter Eleven

Discovering and Assessing Collaboration Engineering Opportunities

Collaboration engineering researchers have developed structured methodologies (Kolfschoten et al., 2006b) and modeling tools (Dean et al., 1994/1995; Dennis et al., 1999; Dean et al., 2000; de Vreede and Briggs, 2005; Kolfschoten et al., 2006a) to support their design efforts. Additionally, they have derived a design pattern language called thinkLets which provides reusable building blocks for designing and training new collaboration processes (Briggs and de Vreede, 2001). However, collaboration engineering field experience shows that, even for a small project, a collaboration engineering intervention may require episodic attention across several months. Collaboration engineering efforts can also require substantial investments of effort and resources. Therefore, assuming that collaboration engineers were able to produce useful designs for new work practices, it would also be valuable if they were able to predict whether such efforts would be likely to result in self-sustaining groups of practitioners for the new work practice.

Previous research from Dean et al. (2006) suggests five criteria for identifying projects that might be conducive to a collaboration engineering intervention. These criteria include the following:

1. Clearly defined outcomes for the collaboration engineering project from the process owner.

2. Important, yet inefficient recurring processes.

3. Tasks of an appropriate type based on the interaction intensity, information processing intensity, and the number of participants.

4. Participants in the task tend to have aligned goals.

5. Champions and adequate budgets.

In this chapter we extend that work by applying the Value Frequency Model (VFM) (Briggs, 2006) for change-of-work-practice to the derivation of an interview protocol for discovering and qualifying collaboration engineering opportunities. We first define key terms and then summarize the propositions of the VFM. We next explain how the questions of the interview protocol link to the constructs of the VFM. We then report the results of two field studies we conducted where people used the protocol to discover and evaluate collaboration engineering opportunities in their own organizations. Finally, the chapter concludes by providing suggestions for future research.

Key Terms and Concepts

As explained in the previous chapter, *collaboration engineering* is an approach to designing collaborative work practices for high-value recurring tasks and transferring them to practitioners to execute for themselves without the ongoing intervention of professional facilitators (de Vreede and Briggs, 2005; Briggs et al., 2006). In that definition, a *work practice* is a customary way of executing a specific organizational task. Therefore, a *change-of-work-practice* is the abandonment of one work practice in favor of another. Changes-of-work-practice could be realized in many ways, including but not limited to changes of goals, deliverables, roles, responsibilities, policies and constraints, procedures, reward structures, data, information, software, and hardware.

Some work practices can be executed by an individual. In such cases, changes-of-practice are a matter of individual choice and unit of analysis would be the individual. However, collaboration engineers design work practices for people who must collaborate. In such cases, the unit of analysis would be the *work group*, or the collection of individuals who must contribute to the successful execution of the new work practice. For the work group unit of analysis, a work practice is defined as having changed when all individuals in the work group have ceased using the old work practice and have begun using the new work practice. If any member of the work group refuses to change to a new work practice, the group as a whole cannot change, because the contributions of all members in a work group are necessary to successful execution of the practice. Thus, for the work group unit of analysis, change-of-practice is defined as a Boolean construct.

A *collaboration engineering opportunity* is a work practice to which the principles and practices of collaboration engineering could be applied in an attempt to improve the effectiveness and efficiency of those who execute it as well as to improve the quality of its deliverables. *Qualifying* a collaboration engineering opportunity means judging the degree to which it seems likely that a work group would become self-sustaining with a new collaborative work practice design for the task, should one be implemented (assuming that the new work practice design is sound). A work group is said to be *self-sustaining* with a work practice if: 1) practitioners continue to use the work practice without ongoing intervention from a change champion, 2) newcomers to the organization are trained in its practice as the standard way of achieving a task, and 3) when problems arise with a work practice or the technologies that support it practitioners remedy the problem rather than abandoning the work practice (Briggs et al., 1998/1999).

The Value Frequency Model

Sometimes innovative work practices catch on and spread quickly, garnering self-sustaining and growing communities of practice. Other times existing work practices remain unchanged or change very slowly, despite strong evidence that available alternatives offer considerable advantages (Corbitt et al., 2000). The VFM (Briggs, 2006) proposes an explanation for variations in the willingness of individuals to change their work practices. The VFM is a modification of the Technology Transition Model (TTM) (Briggs et al., 1998/1999), which was originally proposed explain the use or abandonment of technologies. Over time, the authors of the TTM noted that the model could be applied to the more general construct, change-of-work-practice, and so its consequent construct was broadened and its name changed to reflect its new purpose. In this section, we summarize the propositions of VFM (see Figure 1).

Figure 1. The Propositions of the Value Frequency Model for Change-of-Practice

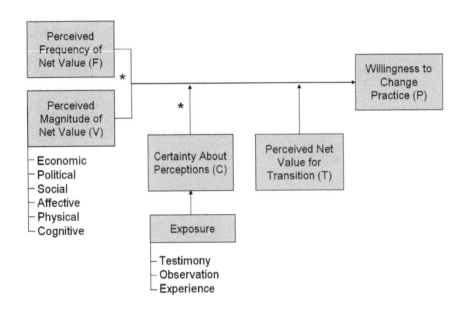

VFM proposes that an individual's willingness to change from current to new work practices is a multiplicative function of the two constructs: 1) perceived magnitude of net value for change and 2) perceived frequency of value after change. *Perceived Magnitude of Net Value* is defined as an overall sense of the degree to which a proposed change would yield overall positive or negative outcomes. VFM posits that people may perceive value along at least six dimensions: economic, political, social, cognitive, affective, and physical dimensions. A proposed change may create positive or negative value along any or all of these dimensions. VFM assumes that a subconscious mechanism synthesizes an overall perception of the degree to which a proposed change would be good or bad for an individual. VFM posits that willingness to change to a new work practice is a function of the degree to which people perceive that making the change would, on the whole, be positive or negative. The more positive is the perceived net value of change, the stronger will be the willingness to change. The more negative is the perceived net value of change, the stronger will be the unwillingness, or resistance to change. The label, perceived magnitude of net value, will be shorted to *perceived value* for the rest of this paper.

Perceived Value is not sufficient to explain change of practice. Some changes are perceived to yield their net value (positive or negative) in a single event. Others are perceived to yield their net value multiple times. VFM proposes that change-of-practice is also a function of *Perceived Frequency of Net Value,* which is defined as an overall sense of how often an individual might attain the positive or negative value ascribed to the proposed change-of-practice To illustrate, one new accounting innovation might create value once a year by simplifying year-end closings, while another accounting innovation might create value daily by eliminating the need to key transactions into the system by hand. The label, perceived frequency of net value will be shorted to *perceived frequency* for the balance of this paper.

VFM proposes change of practice as a multiplicative function of both perceived value and perceived frequency. By this reasoning, people could feel equal willingness toward a change where they perceived the potential for small value on a frequent basis as for a change where they perceive large benefit on an infrequent basis. For the balance of this chapter, we will refer to this multiplicative relationship between perceived value and perceived frequency as a *value-frequency judgment*.

VFM goes on to posit that the primary causal relationship between the value-frequency judgment and change-of-practice is moderated by two other constructs: 1) *certainty about perceptions* and 2) *perceived net value of transition* (Briggs, 2006). *Certainty about perceptions* is defined as a subconscious assessment of the likelihood that an individual's value and frequency perceptions are accurate. It could be instantiated as a continuous variable that takes a value ranging from zero to one, where zero means that people have no confidence that their value and frequency perceptions are warranted, and one means that people are fully certain of their value and frequency perceptions.

VFM posits that certainty comes from exposure to the proposed work practice. Exposure may take at least three forms: 1) *testimonial*, 2) *observation*, or 3) *experience* (Briggs, 2006). After a glowing pitch from a change champion, for example, people might perceive potential for great value in a proposed new practice, but lacking information about the credibility of the champion and the details of the proposed practice, they may feel uncertain that such value could actually be realized. Observing others who are using the proposed practice, or actually testing the new practice for themselves, may increase the degree to which they feel certain about their value-frequency judgments.

The *Perceived net value of transition* construct is defined as an overall sense of the positive or negative value that would derive from the change process itself. For example, an individual might regard training sessions for the proposed work practice as a negative cognitive interference with other priorities. On the other hand, they might regard a trip to Hawaii in January to take the training as having positive physical, social, and affective value. If the perceived net value of transition is sufficiently negative, it can overwhelm a positive value-frequency judgment, resulting in an overall unwillingness to make a change-of-practice.

It is important to note that VFM does not posit that perceived-net-value-of-transition would occur at a later time than the value-frequency judgment. Rather, it posits that, at a given moment in time, individuals hold both a value-frequency judgment and a perception of net value for transition. It posits that, should there be shifts with respect to those constructs at any time, then there would also be shifts in willingness to change.

Interview Protocol Development

We used the constructs and propositions of VFM as the starting point for deriving an interview protocol to help identify and assess collaboration engineering opportunities. The specifics of the protocol were further informed by our use of preliminary versions of the questions in the field with people from commercial, government, military, and organizations. The goal of the interview protocol reported in this paper is to provide collaboration engineers with insight about the degree to which a group may need - and may be willing to accept - a change-of practice. It seeks to rule out collaboration engineering opportunities for which there is low likelihood for change-of-work-practice, even if a better work practice were to be designed.

The Collaboration Engineering Opportunity Interview Protocol incorporates two layers of questions. The first layer of questions seeks to surface collaboration engineering opportunities. The second seeks to evaluate the likelihood that, for a given opportunity, a sound collaboration engineering solution could successfully attract a self-sustaining community of practitioners. This section discusses the derivation of the protocol.

Protocol for Discovering Collaboration Engineering Opportunities

The first layer of the interview protocol has five parts. We discuss each part in this section. The full first layer of the protocol appears below.

Establish Common Meaning

1. People apply many different meanings to the word 'collaboration.' When you say 'collaboration' what do you mean?
    a. When we speak of 'collaboration' we mean a "joint effort toward a common goal."

Identify Candidate Practices

2. Do you or your people have any important recurring tasks where they must work in a group to create a joint deliverable?
    a. How are these tasks going?
    b. Are any of these processes good candidates for enhancement or improvement?
3. Are there other high-utility activities that require the efforts of a group on a regular basis?
    a. How are those processes working for you?
    b. Are they painful processes?

Discovering Opportunities for Improvement

4. What are the toughest tasks you or your people have to do in a group?
5. What other group tasks give you or your people the most trouble?

Other People's Challenges

6. Who else do you know that has a tough collaboration challenge?
7. Do you know any other groups who must work together frequently, who may hate some part of their task?

Prioritization / Direction

8. Reviewing the processes we've talked about, which is THE one? THE three?
    a. We've heard about (X) processes from you. Would you please rate these work practices with an A, B, C, or Z? (A = very high priority, B = Medium Priority, C = Low priority, Z = Don't want to touch it)

Questions to Establish Shared Understanding. In pilot testing the protocol, it was discovered that it was useful to open a collaboration engineering interview by explicitly stating its goals. Otherwise, it was found that the first interview question tended to elicit long, vague monologues on tangentially related topics. The protocol therefore opens with the following statement:

As collaboration engineers, we apply the findings of collaboration science to the design and deployment of new collaborative work practices supported by appropriate technologies.

For certain kinds of collaborative tasks we can cut work hours in half and cut task cycle times by 50-

75%, while improving the detail and quality of deliverables.

We are looking for opportunities to work with groups who could benefit from judicious applications of our collaboration techniques and technologies.

One way we can make a substantial difference is to focus on high-value recurring collaborative tasks.

We're trying to find specific groups that work on specific jobs to create defined deliverables, who might welcome the opportunity to work with us to enhance their performance and satisfaction.

We also learned that people hold a wide range of different definitions for the term, *collaboration.* **Interviewees defined in various ways, for example,**

"Software technology for exchanging files."

"Sharing resources."

"Including everybody in the decision."

We therefore ask the following question as our first question:

1. *We have learned that people apply a lot of different meanings to the word, "collaboration." As a start, we'd like to learn your definition and to tell you ours. When you say, "collaboration," what do you mean?*

We follow the interviewee's response with the following statement:

When we speak of collaboration, we mean, "joint effort toward a group goal for mutual benefit." Does that definition make sense to you?

All interviewees in the study found this definition to be clear and deemed the definition to be acceptable in the context of the interview.

Questions for Identifying Candidate Practices. VFM posits that in order for a change-of-work-practice to occur, practitioners must perceive positive utility would accrue from making the change. Processes which are painful, unpleasant, and inefficient would offer opportunities for larger perceived utility than would processes that are deemed by their practitioners to be effective, efficient, and satisfying.

It was discovered however, that interviewees were reluctant to air their process-related problems early in the interview. We therefore began the next phase with questions about high-value recurring work practices and neutral questions about how well those processes worked:

2. *Do you or your people have any important recurring tasks where they must work in a group to create a joint deliverable?*

    a. *How are these tasks going?*

    b. *Are any of these processes good candidates for enhancement or improvement?*

3. *Are there other high-utility activities that require the efforts of a group on a regular basis?*

    a. *How are those processes working for you?*

    b. *Are they painful in any way?*

In the field, it was found that it typically took about a half-hour for participants to respond to this set of questions. Note that the last question in the block broaches the question of pain for the first time.

Questions for Discovering Opportunities for Improvement. Having discussed collaborative processes in general, the next block of questions specifically asks about processes that are not going well and which may therefore be candidates for collaboration engineering interventions, because they may constitute an opportunity to invoke a positive value-frequency judgment for a proposed change. The goal of these questions is to get a sense of how interviewees may perceive the magnitude of value that might be obtained from changing a practice. Specifically, asking about their toughest problems leads toward addressing practices with the highest utility:

4. *What are the toughest tasks you or your people have to do in a group?*

5. *What other group tasks give you or your people the most trouble?*

Questions for Discovering Other People's Collaboration Challenges. After exploring the state of processes in the interviewee's domain, the protocol asks whether they know of challenging collaboration processes outside their own domain. The rationale for these questions is very similar to the rationale provided above, in that they seek to uncover work practices where opportunities may exist to create a positive value-frequency judgment for a proposed change. However, the difference here is that the questions focus on other people's process problems rather than those of the interviewee. The protocol questions for this section are as follows:

6. *Who else do you know that has a tough collaboration challenge?*

7. *Do you know any other groups who must work together frequently, who may hate some part of their task?*

Protocol for Screening Collaboration Engineering Opportunities

Whenever the questions in the first layer of the protocol reveal a candidate work practice the interviewer shifts to the second layer of questions to evaluate the likelihood that an intervention could lead to a sustained change-of-work-practice. The second layer of the protocol addresses eleven topics to the interviewee. We learned that interviewees frequently misunderstand the wording of a question the first time it is asked, so we framed two different questions for each topic. The full text of the second layer of the protocol appears in Appendix B.

Questions of Process Frequency. VFM posits that change-of-work-practice is a function of the frequency with which people perceive they will obtain utility from the new practice. The first two screening questions are therefore:

1. *How frequently is this task executed?*

2. *How often does the group meet to do this task?*

Questions of Individual Frequency. An interviewee was once asked how frequently a task was executed and received the reply, "200 times per year." All other screening criteria came out in favor of conducting a collaboration engineering intervention, so we began the project. We were weeks into the effort before we learned that 200 different people executed the process once-a-year each. The target practitioners perceived a positive net value in the proposed change, but did not perceive that they would receive that value sufficiently frequently to be worth learning the new practice. They judged that they would be likely forget the details of the new practice from year to year, and so would have to relearn it each time. In order to screen for tasks that may have a low perceived-frequency-of-net-value, we added the following questions to the protocol:

3. *Do the same individuals execute or lead this task again and again? How often?*

4. *Is this a task that recurs for the same person?*

5. *How frequently?*

Questions of High Utility. VFM posits that people must perceive utility in the proposed new work practice. An improvement to a task that creates great benefit for an organization might be perceived as creating more utility than an improvement to a task that creates minor benefit. So, while the interviewee had identified troublesome or tough tasks in the Layer 1 questions, it is useful to try to extract an estimate of the utility they might realize from improving that task. Within our application of the protocol, this information proved useful in prioritizing candidate tasks for improvement. We therefore ask:

6. *What is the payoff if this task goes well? Who gets that payoff?*

7. *What's the down side if this task goes badly or fails? Who pays that price?*

Questions of Work Group Size. The more people are involved in a collaborative task the more benefit the techniques of collaboration engineering can provide and the people there will be who perceive those benefits. We therefore ask:

8. *How many people are involved in the execution of this task?*

9. *Who are they?*

10. *What roles do they take?*

Questions of Duration. The longer a task takes the greater will be the benefit of reducing its execution cycle, and so the greater will be the opportunity to create a positive perception of net value for a new work practice. Similarly, experience has shown that the longer a task takes, the more likely it was that a collaboration engineering intervention could make improvements to cycle times. We therefore ask:

11. *How long does a typical session take?*

12. *What's the range of durations for this task?*

13. Is every role in for the duration?

14. How many hours/days does each role spend?

Questions of Affective Response to Task. Half the people who execute a task find it unpleasant in some way then there are greater opportunities to demonstrate the utility of a proposed change than if the practitioners find the task pleasant. Likewise, if there is an element of the task the practitioners find particularly pleasant, then it would be useful for the collaboration engineering to seek to retain that aspect in the new work practice, or to replace it with something more pleasant. We therefore ask:

15. How do people feel about the process?

16. Do they love life or hate life when they have to do this task? Why?

17. Is there any part of this task that people especially like or dislike? Why?

Questions of Goals and Deliverables. In order to gain a more detailed understanding of the utility that a task creates for an organization and the degree to which collaboration engineering might be able to assist a group in successfully completing the task, we ask the interviewee:

18. What important goals or outcomes for this task could be improved?

19. What are the deliverables for this task? How do those deliverables serve the interests of the stakeholders for this task?

Questions of Resistance to Change. Many of the other questions in the protocol seek information that points to opportunities to create positive utility by changing a work practice. Negative utility however, is also a possible outcome for a change. The following questions help assess the perceived utility of the change and also begin to examine the perceived utility of the transition. We therefore ask:

20. What are the drivers that keep the process as it is today?

21. Who would pay what kind of price if you were to change to a new process?

Questions of Leadership. If there is already someone whose job title or job description requires that they execute a task, then there will be someone whose performance evaluations depend on the success of the task. Such individuals may therefore have a direct stake in the value-frequency outcomes a new work practice could provide. They may therefore choose to advocate for a change should a better work practice be proposed. Leaders of such tasks may also be able to shift the value-frequency judgments of other practitioners by tying positive political, economic, affective, social, or other utility to a transition to the new work practice. For example, systems analysts are responsible for conducting requirements negotiations and so a senior analyst can take charge of assuring that all analysts under his or her leadership learn the new approach. On the other hand, if no identifiable person is in charge of a task there will be nobody to champion and oversee the change. For example, a number of our interviewees wanted to "improve meetings." However, in most organizations, there is no czar in charge of meetings who could oversee and motivate the deployment of new meeting practices. The answers to these types of questions help determine whether the change in practice is likely to be sustained over the long term. We therefore ask:

22. *Whose job is it to lead this task?*

23. *Who owns this task?*

Questions of Resources. If a budget is already allocated to a task this is an indicator of the value an organization ascribes to the task. It also means that there may be measurable monetary value from improving the task and that there may be resources available to support a collaboration engineering intervention. We therefore ask:

24. *Is there already a budget in place to execute this task?*

25. *Is it sufficient?*

Questions of Generalizability. If the same process design could be used by many different work groups, then an improved process is likely to generate more value and that value is likely to be perceived by more people than if the process will only be executed by a single work group. We therefore ask:

26. *How many other groups could use variations on this process if we were to develop it?*

27. *Are there other tasks that could use the same process?*

Questions of Capability and Capacity. In addition to the questions the collaboration engineers ask the interviewees, the protocol contains two questions that the collaboration engineers may ask themselves about their own capabilities and capacity to implement a solution for the opportunity:

28. *(Internal) Can we readily help with the expertise we already know?*

29. *(Internal) Can we complete the intervention in a timely manner?*

Interviewee Priorities

The final questions the interview protocol asks about the relative priority the interviewee ascribes to the opportunities identified and evaluated during the session. These questions give another indication of the relative value-frequency judgments the interviewee may ascribe to improving the candidate processes. Further, we learned in the field that addressing high-value, high-priority tasks early in a working relationship helps improve support for subsequent collaboration engineering efforts. Therefore, we ask:

1. *Reviewing the candidate processes we've talked about during this interview, which is would you say is the single most important one to improve?*

2. *Which are the three most important?*

3. *We've heard about (some number of) processes from you. Would you please rate each these work practices with an A, B, C, or Z?*

    a. *An "A" means very important*

    b. *A "B" means moderately important*

    c. *A "C" means not very important*

    d. *A "Z" means there are political or other factors that suggest any attempt to change this process would fail*

Field Study Results

The interview protocol was tested with two different groups; a group of experienced collaboration engineers working in a large, global organization and a group of knowledge workers with no previous collaboration engineering experience, who worked with a collection of for-profit and non-profit organizations. For this study, an action-research approach was applied. With action research, one starts with a theory and intervenes in a situation to improve both the situation and the theory (Argyris et al.,

1982). We began with VFM and worked directly with people in the organization to improve the likelihood that new work practices would successfully transition to the practitioners. We report critical incidents and outcomes of two studies in the following sections.

Study 1: A Multi-National Organization

In this study, the protocol was used to interview 17 senior executives in the headquarters operation of a large multi-national organization. About 3000 people work in the headquarters operation. The research team consisted of a scheduler, lead interviewer, scribe, second interviewer, and a reviewer. The scheduler coordinated calendars, made appointments, and rescheduled appointments as they were postponed or cancelled. The interviewer and second interviewer posed questions from the protocol to the interviewee and conversed with the interviewee about their responses. The scribe listened to the interview and made more-detailed notes about questions and responses, but occasionally also asked questions for clarification or follow-up. The role of the scribe was especially important as the research team was unable to rely on any recording or other electronic devices during the interviews. Additionally, the other team members made notes as time permitted. Upon completion of each interview, the interview team met and consolidated their notes onto a single detailed narrative of the interview. The reviewer read the transcript and checked it for clarity, completeness, correctness, and consistency. Table 1 is an example from a final transcript of the first layer of the interview protocol for one such interview.

Table 1. Final Transcript of Opportunity Discovery Protocol

1. *People apply many different meanings to the word 'collaboration.' When you say 'collaboration' what do you mean?*

   a. In response to the first of the protocol questions the interviewee defined collaboration as "two or more people coming together to reach a similar goal or outcome." We took some time to let him know what we mean and clarified any inconsistencies. Specifically stating that when we speak of 'collaboration' we mean a "joint effort toward a common goal." The interviewee accepted that definition without reservations.

2. *Do you or your people have any important recurring tasks where they must work in a group to create a joint deliverable? How are these tasks going? Are any of these processes good candidates for enhancement or improvement?*

   a. In response to this question, the interviewee stated that his groups need help planning a project. Specifically the interviewee recalled that his IT group needs help in establishing a process to put together a training program for knowledge management. He described the project planning task as a task that happens weekly or bi-weekly including 8-12 or sometimes 15 individuals. The team gets together to identify action items. Currently the team struggles with group dynamics and figuring out what needs to be done. The interviewee stated that as a team, they don't know what they need to accomplish and they don't work together in sharing the information about how to move forward.

3. *Are there other high-utility activities that require the efforts of a group on a regular basis? How are those processes working for you? Are they painful processes?*

   a. In response to this question, the interviewee stated that other than needing help with project planning, his team needs help regarding a process for identifying requirements. He stated that they want to have information access based on their position in the organization. Currently, the team is working on a plan to have a hierarchy system and not three different systems. The interviewee stated that these meetings again have between 8-12 people talking about the requirements to make this happen.

4. *What are the toughest tasks you or your people have to do in a group?*

a. The toughest task identified by the interviewee is the management of the organization's information. The head of the organization is frustrated with not being able to identify the information he wants to know. The interviewee stated that the organizational members need all the information and the ability to drill down with a web service in a shorter time. They struggle with creating a 'flatter' organization.

5. *What other group tasks give you or your people the most trouble?*

a. This question resulted in response to the task of problem identification and injection. Currently, the interviewee does not know how problems are identified for him and his people to work on. For the most part, the head of the organization says "work on this" and that is what they work on. The interviewee stated that there is a group meeting every week with between 8-12 people who define the role of the team. This team suffers from inefficient meetings. Then 6-8 people get together to put together an action plan. With the current process, they team discusses for an hour and ends up with no action items. The interviewee stated that it is both a process and a culture issue. "It is a process issue because there is either no process or a lack of process and it is a culture issue because

people are coming to the meetings with no expectation of reaching an answer or deliverable."

6. *Who else do you know that has a tough collaboration challenge?*

a. In response to this question, the interviewee stated that every team in the organization could benefit from an after action review process. He suggested that this would be helpful for making sure that the processes are being used. For example, at the end of every day team members could report on what they had accomplished, what they did well, what they had done poorly, where they had been lucky, where they had been unlucky, and what they would do differently another time. Otherwise, this could be completed once or twice a week instead of every night.

7. *Do you know any other groups who must work together frequently, who may hate some part of their task?*

a. Another group that the interviewee identified is the requirements review board (RRB) whom he heard has a painful process. He said that this meeting involves about 20 people each time and they meet about once a month.

8. *Reviewing the processes we've talked about, which is THE one? THE three?*

    a. Ideally the interviewee said that he would be happy if processes could be created that increase both team productivity and satisfaction. He said that no longer hearing people after meetings say "that was a waste of time" would be great.

9. *We've heard about seven processes from you. Would you please rate these work practices with an A, B, C, or Z? (A = very high priority, B = Medium Priority, C = Low priority, Z = Don't want to touch it)*

    a. The interviewee rated the process of information access = A, project planning = B, communities of interest = C for some, A for others, RRB = B, group tasks = A, auditing = B, and problem acceptance = A.

The 17 original interviews with senior executives and managers yielded 30 potential collaboration engineering opportunities. Of these candidates, interviewees characterized 14 as 'A' or very important, four were classified as 'B' or moderately important, six were classified as 'C' or not very important, and six were put into the 'Z' category.

The organization's requirements definition process was a good example of a 'Z' rated process. Many interviewees reported that the process was very important, very painful, and badly broken. However, they also reported that powerful interests within the organization were deliberately subverting the process to keep their own domains running smoothly. They suggested that any attempt to fix the process would be likely to produce obstruction at best and retribution at worst, with little chance of producing meaningful change. Within the terminology of VFM, this equated to high potential of negative political value, even potentially extending to negative economic consequences. Together, these effects dramatically reduced perceptions of net value for this initiative for most interviewees. That project therefore warranted a Z classification. Thus, attention was directed to processes whose stakeholders perceived a positive value-frequency judgment for change.

Selecting a Candidate for Implementation

To test whether the information yielded by the protocol was a useful way to predict whether a collaboration engineering intervention might succeed, all 30 candidate processes were re-evaluated to find one that produced strongly positive indicators for most of the questions in the protocol. The organization's staff meeting process surfaced as the strongest candidate. Almost all members of the organization participated in one or more staff meetings per week. Many participated in at least two; one with their subordinates and another with their superior. Thus, an engineered process would be generalizable to many different work groups and any positive utility they would derive from an improvement would be realized more frequently than for most of the other candidate tasks. All interviewees who discussed staff meetings reported feeling that staff meetings were very important to the success of the organization, but were mostly a waste of time for the 8-12 participants. These individuals typically sat through about 90-120 minutes of status reports by others waiting for their own chance to brief their leader for a few minutes. Further, they were always required to stop work that they deemed to be more meaningful in order to prepare PowerPoint slides for these meetings. Interviewees reported feeling bored and annoyed. The first interviewee expressed a desire for these meetings to become active sessions where participants helped one another solve problems or improve their likelihood of success. Subsequent interviewees expressed similar sentiments. However, leaders needed to know project and action item status and they believed that the meetings would have to retain their declarative nature. Thus, there was a felt pain and an eagerness for change, but no insights about how such a change could be effected.

There were people whose job it was to run these meetings and each practitioner ran them repeatedly, so there was someone who could adopt an engineered approach if one were offered. There was not, however a line item in the budget so few resources were available to support an implementation for such a project, thus any solution would have to be fast to design and have virtually no cost to implement.

Participants did not want to devote any more time to staff meetings than they were already spending. However, they also did not want to give up regular meetings with their superiors. Several reported that one's status and power in the organization was largely a function of "face-time," the number of hours per week one spent with ones boss. So they did not want to eliminate the meetings, only to change their nature in order to make them more productive. Within the terminology of VFM, this equated to high potential of positive economic and cognitive effects.

Implementing a collaboration engineering Solution

We designed a new work practice that would make the recording of status update information into an asynchronous, pre-meeting, online activity that would run continuously throughout the week. For each project, people would record 1) project milestones, 2) accomplishments this period, 3) actions next period, and 4) issues and barriers to their success. When the groups met face-to-face, they would be expected to have already read the on-line status reports. They would focus their face-to-face discussions on helping to resolve one another's barriers or issues, changing the staff meeting into a problem-solving session rather than a briefing.

Deploying the New Work Practice

Our first indication that the new approach might, in fact, transition successfully to practitioners happened during our first design meeting. When we met with our first change champion, several people from another part of the organization sat in as observers to learn more about collaboration engineering. During the design meeting, the observers became excited as the design unfolded. They engaged in animated conversations among themselves about how they could implement the design in their own work group. They argued in a friendly but forceful manner with the collaboration engineers that the design should be changed in ways that would better suit their own needs. The collaboration engineers had to remind them several times that they were, in fact, observers and that the needs of the change champion had to prevail in this meeting.

Interestingly, within two days of the design meeting, the observers implemented a variation on the design for themselves, while the original client could not mount a successful implementation. The original change champion found himself caught in the crossfire of a political battle between two other powerful individuals. Their dispute had nothing to do with staff meetings, but the implementation of the new staff meeting process became the focal point of their conflict.

Other work groups in the organization heard about the successful implementation by the observer group and contacted the research team to learn more about it. We created a reusable presentation to explain the new approach. We created process documentation and training materials people could use to implement the approach for themselves. Within 3 months, about 75 headquarter personnel were using the approach for their staff meetings.

Several groups attempted to use the new approach, but did not succeed. Three groups tried to use the supporting technology we had configured without first learning the process the technology was meant to support. All three declared the approach to be useless and abandoned their attempt to implement. We interviewed the leaders of all three groups about their decisions. They reported that the new approach would require extra work without providing benefit. All assumed that the contents of the online postings would have to be manually ported into a PowerPoint presentation and that staff meetings would proceed in their usual format – each person taking a turn to brief their leader. This constituted a perception of negative cognitive value for the proposed change. Further, they reported that the supporting software behaved in ways that didn't make sense to them – a negatively-perceived cognitive value – and so it wasn't worth learning. Thus, consistent with the theory, these users perceived a negative net value for the proposed change of practice, and chose not to make the change. Drawing further on the theory, we sought to create interventions that would shift the value-frequency judgment toward the positive. We explained that the new approach was more than a technology; it was a new process, a new way of keeping leaders updated on project status. It was not meant to add to the existing staff meeting process, it was meant to replace it. We offered a one hour training session to clarify both the process and the tools. One group accepted the training and became self-sustaining practitioners. The other two declined the training and did not adopt.

Two other groups that took the training and started using the process with enthusiasm later reported that it created too much work for them. When we investigated, we learned that their leaders had decided that PowerPoint slides were sufficiently important that the group had to both update the online system and make slides before each meeting. Further, they had to deliver their usual briefings at the staff meetings rather than focusing their efforts on devising creative solutions to one another's challenges. The leaders both reported that it was easier for them to listen to briefings from slides than to read the status updates on line before the meeting. One reported that he was too busy to read the online updates before the meeting. The other reported that he needed the slides from his subordinates so he could use them for presentations to his superiors. For these groups, the new approach delivered negative value rather than positive value. The leaders created negative political utility for abandoning the old practice. The new practice therefore created negative cognitive utility for its practitioners because it required extra attention without relieving the burdens of the old practice. Both groups abandoned the new approach. In both cases, the refusal of one member of the work group to adopt the new work practice blocked the whole work group from such adoption. The leader's decisions created perceptions of negative political value for continuing the new practice, and negative cognitive value for combining the old and new practices. The groups therefore reverted to their old practices.

Among other groups that investigated, but did not adopt the new process, the most frequently reported concern had to do with visibility and accountability. They candidly reported that they did not want others outside their group to know exactly what they were doing, and how they were doing it, especially their bosses. Their concerns were that: 1) others would dispute their goals or methods, 2) others might use the information in an attempt to acquire their resources, and 3) their bosses might use the information as a basis for inflicting negative consequences on them. For these groups, the potential political risks outweighed the potential reductions of cognitive load and time savings the new process could provide. Thus, they perceived a net negative value for making the change.

Currently, nine months into the project, we regularly receive one to two queries a week from new groups at headquarters who wish to learn the new staff meeting practice. About half of those typically attempt a pilot implementation. Almost all groups that implement ask for minor revisions to the process and to the configuration of the supporting technology to adapt it to their own ways of working. The earliest adopters of the new process were typically groups led by middle and senior managers. We have recently begun to receive queries from the offices of the most senior executives in the organization about implementing the practice for their direct reports. Should these people adopt the practice, this may create positive political and cognitive value for the direct reports to implement the process with their own subordinates.

In this case, the data obtained with the collaboration engineering interview protocol provided a prediction that was born out in practice – consistent with VFM, the new staff meeting process appears to have garnered a self-sustaining and growing community of practice among some users. Further, the choices of specific groups who chose not to adopt the new practice could also be explained in terms of VFM. Thus, the research provides some support for both the theory and the interview protocol.

Study 2: Knowledge Workers without Collaboration Engineering Experience

Having demonstrated with that we could use a the protocol to select a project with a potential to succeed at the organizational level, and that we could explain the cases where it did and did didn't succeed at the work group level, we wanted to learn whether that success was dependent on our expertise, or whether it could be replicated by others with less experience. We therefore worked with a group of 33 knowledge workers who were just beginning to learn the principles of collaboration engineering. Six of these worked in the financial services industry, four worked for a large transportation company, one worked for a large government contractor; two were consultants in private practice, and the rest worked for a variety of for-profit and non-profit organizations. We briefed the novices on the interview protocol and asked them to use it to discover two candidate tasks for collaboration engineering in their own organizations and to fully evaluate one of the candidates in terms of the protocol and to deliver a two-page analysis and recommendation. Four participants opted out of the task. The other 29 completed the task successfully; 25 of them in commercial businesses and 4 non-profit organizations. Of the 29 opportunities, 9 yielded negative indicators for most questions and the novices recommended against pursuing the opportunities. In one such case, for example, the proposed project focused on an employee review process for a national auto parts retailer. The process involved only three people and lasted only four-to-five minutes. During this process the group created no deliverables and the process occurred about once per month. Thus, the value-frequency judgment was low. In another, an electric utility company had what appeared to be a collaborative process for allocating work orders. However further investigation revealed that, although the process involved a group, it was not collaborative because a single expert told the others what to do.

Two experienced collaboration engineers on our research team read the analyses delivered by the novices and made their own recommendations. In all cases, the recommendations of the novices about whether to move forward with a project matched those of the experienced collaboration engineers.

Sixteen of the novices broke into five teams and developed simple solutions for the five most-promising opportunities. They briefed their solutions to one another and to us and revised their designs based on the feedback they received. They then proposed their solutions to the managers in the organizations. Four of the five were accepted for implementation. One of those implementations is completed at the time of this writing, and appears to have garnered a self-sustaining community of practitioners. Another implementation within a consultancy became the stimulus for a larger-scale redesign of work practices, and led the organization to make substantial revisions to the software they use to support their practices. The other two implementations are still in progress. These findings suggest that novices may be able to use the protocol to identify candidate tasks for collaboration engineering interventions and to derive useful recommendations for or against proceeding with a collaboration engineering project based on their findings.

Summary

This chapter highlighted fundamental principles and the field test results of an interview protocol based on VFM informed by field experience which was designed to discover and assess collaboration engineering opportunities in order to predict whether such efforts were likely to yield a successful transition to the new work practice. Adoptions and non-adoptions of the new staff-meeting work practice were consistent with the model from which the protocol was developed. Reports of positive value-frequency judgments from potential practitioners did coincide with adoptions of the new work practice. Reports of negative value-frequency judgments coincided with decisions not to implement the new practice. Reports of negative value-frequency judgments that arose after implementation coincided with decisions to revert to former practices. These outcomes are consistent with the propositions of VFM. Furthermore, the degree to which the interview protocol presaged the likely success of the new staff meeting approach suggests at a minimum that it may be worthwhile to pursue tests of the protocol and of VFM over a longer time frame with a wider variety of work practices.

In the second phase of the study, where novice collaboration engineers applied the interview protocol, the success with which novice collaboration engineers were able to identify and evaluate candidate tasks for collaboration engineering interventions further suggests that at least some merit rests in the protocol itself, rather than solely in the experts who deployed it in the first study. This suggests that, after further testing, the interview protocol may become a useful tool for the collaboration engineering community. Beyond its utility as a protocol, it may also be a useful device for training collaboration engineers how to discover and assess opportunities to apply their approach.

This study has several limitations that should be kept in mind. First we tested the protocol by attempting interventions that received positive indicators, and indeed, those interventions appear to be succeeding consistent with the predictions of VFM. In order to test the theory more fully using the collaboration engineering Interview protocol, it would be necessary to attempt to implement solutions both where the theory predicts success and where it predicts failure. However, it would be unethical to encourage an organization to devote resources to designing and deploying a practice that is likely to fail. We were able to bypass this constraint to some extent by tracking the progress of specific groups within the organization that both chose to adopt and chose not to adopt the same new practice. To further overcome this constraint, researchers may wish to pay special attention to projects where an organization insists on implementing a collaboration engineering solution, even though interview results suggests the effort is likely to fail. Such cases would provide a basis strong basis for comparison without violating ethical considerations.

That said, our experience with the protocol in multiple settings under varying conditions suggest that interview protocol may be a useful tool for making such predictions and that the theory from which it is derived may be a useful model for coming to understand the change-of-work-practice phenomena. Our attempt to apply the theory in the field, informed by empirical and pragmatic considerations yielded an approach to assessing the potential for success in a collaboration engineering initiative could help collaboration engineering's focus where initiatives are most likely to return utility for the effort expended.

References

Aalst, W.M.P van der; Hofstede, A.H.M. ter and Kiepuszewski, B. (2003). Workflow Patterns, Distributed and Parallel Databases 14: 5-51.

Abelson, R. P. 1981. Psychological status of the script concept. American Psychologist 36, no. 7: 715–729.

Ackermann, F. (1996), 'Participants' Perceptions on the Role of Facilitators Using Group Decision Support Systems'. Group Decision and Negotiation, No. 5, 93-112.

Agres, A., Vreede, G.J., de and Briggs, R.O. (2005) A Tale of Two Cities: Case Studies of GSS Transition in Two Organizations, Group Decision and Negotiation, 14,(4).

Aldag, R. J., & Fuller, S. R. (1993). Beyond fiasco: A reappraisal of the groupthink phenomenon and a new model of group decision processes. Psychology Bulletin, 113, 533-552.

Alexander, C. (1979) The Timeless Way of Building, Oxford University Press, New York.

Alexander, C. (1980) The nature of Order: an essay on the art of building and the nature of the universe, The center for environmental structure, Berkeley.

Alexander, C. (1996) Key note at the ACM conference 1996, IEEE Computer Society press, http://www.patternlanguage.com/archive/ieee/ieeetext.htm.

Alexander, C., Ishikawa, S., Silverstein, M., Jacobson, M., Fiksdahl-King, I., Angel, S. (1977) A Pattern Language, Towns, Buildings, Construction, Oxford University Press, New York.

Anson, R., Bostrom, R., Wynne, B. (1995), 'An Experiment Assessing GSS and Facilitator Effects on Meeting Outcomes'. Management Science, 41(2), 189-208.

Appelman, J.H., Driel, J. van (2005), Crisis-response in the Port of Rotterdam: Can we do without a facilitator in distributed settings?, Proceedings of the 38th Hawaii International Conference on System Sciences, IEEE Computer Society Press.

Applegate, L. (1991).Technology support for cooperative work. Journal of Organizational Computing, 1(1),11-39.

Architecture for GSS: Americas Conference on Information Systems (AMCIS). Indianapolis, IN, pp 182-184.

Argyris, C., R. Putnam, D. McLain Smith (1982) Action science - Concepts, methods and skills for research and intervention. San Francisco, Jossey-Bass.

Baltes, B.B., Dickson, M.W., Sherman, M.P., Bauer, C.C., & LaGanke, J.S. (2002). Computer-Mediated Communication and Group

Barzilay, R., McKeown, K.R., & Elhadad, M. 1999. Information Fusion in the Context of Multi-Document Summarization. Paper presented at the Annual meeting of the Association for Computational Linguistics on Computational Linguistics, College Park, Maryland, USA.

Bikson, T.K. (1996). Groupware at the World Bank in Ciborra, C.U.. Groupware and Teamwork - Invisible Aid or Technical Hindrance?, John Wiley & Sons, Chichester, UK, 145-183.

Bock, G. W, R. W Zamud, Y. G Kim, and J. N Lee. 2005. "Behavioral Intention Formation in Knowledge Sharing: Examining the Roles of Extrinsic Motivators, Social-Psychological Forces, and Organizational Climate." Management Information Systems Quarterly (29:1) pp. 87-111.

Boehm, B., Grünbacher, P., Briggs, R.O. (2001), Developing Groupware for Requirements Negotiation: Lessons Learned, IEEE Software, May/June, 46-55.

Bos, N., A. Zimmerman, J. Olson, J. Yew, J. Yerkie, E. Dahl, and G. Olson. 2007. From shared databases to communities of practice: A taxonomy of collaboratories. Journal of Computer-Mediated Communication 12, no. 2: 652–672.

Bostrom, R. P., Anson, R. and Clawson, V. K. (1993) Group facilitation and group support systems, in Jessup, L. M. and Valacich, J. (Eds.) Group support systems: New perspectives, Macmillan, New York, 146-168.

Bragge, J.H., Hengst, M. den, Tuunanen, T., Virtanen, V. (2005), A Repeatable Collaboration Process for Developing a Road Map for Emerging New Technology Business: Case Mobile Marketing, Proceedings of AMCIS 2005, Omaha, NE.

Briggs, R., D. Mittleman, E. Santanen, D. Gillman (1997) Collaborative Molecules: A Component-Based

Briggs, R.O., G.L. Kolfschoten, G.-J. de Vreede, D.L. Dean (2006) Defining key concepts for collaboration engineering: 12th Americas Conference on Information Systems (AMCIS-12). Acapulco, Mexico.

Briggs, R. O. and Vreede, G. J. de. 2001. ThinkLets: Building Blocks for Concerted Collaboration. Tucson, Arizona: GroupSystems Corporation.

Briggs, R. O., & Reinig, B.A. (2007). Bounded Ideation Theory: A New Model of the Relationship between Idea Quantity and Idea-quality during Ideation. Paper presented at the Hawaii International Conference on System Science, Waikoloa.

Briggs, R. O., B. A. Reinig, and G. J. De Vreede. 2008. The yield shift theory of satisfaction and its application to the IS/IT domain. Journal of the AIS 9, no. 5: 267–93.

Briggs, R. O., Davis, A. J., Murphy, J. D., Steinhauser, L. and Carlisle, T. 2007. "Transferring a Collaborative Work Practice to Practitioners: A Field Study of the Value Frequency Model for Change-of-Practice." In J. Haake, S. Ochoa, and A. Cechich (eds.), Lecture Notes on Computer Science. New York: Springer. pp. 295-302.

Briggs, R. O., Kolfschoten, G. L. and Vreede, G. J. 2005. "Toward a Theoretical Model of Consensus Building," AMCIS 2005 Proceedings, Association for information systems, pp. 101-110.

Briggs, R. O., Reinig, B. A. and Vreede, G. J. de. 2008. "The Yield Shift Theory of Satisfaction and its Application to the IS/IT Domain," Journal of the Association for Information Systems (9:5), pp. 267-293.

Briggs, R. O., Vreede, G. J. de and Nunamaker, J. F. Jr. 2003. "Collaboration Engineering with ThinkLets to Pursue Sustained Success with Group Support Systems," Journal of Management Information Systems (19:4), pp. 31-64.

Briggs, R., de Vreede G.J. de (1997), 'Measuring satisfaction in GSS meetings', Proceedings of the 18th ICIS, 486-484.

Briggs, R.O. & de Vreede, G.J. (2009). ThinkLets: Building Blocks for Concerted Collaboration. Delft: Delft University of Technology.

Briggs, R.O. (1994) The focus theory of team productivity and its application to development and testing of electronic group support systems, Tucson.

Briggs, R.O. (1994). The Focus Theory of Team Productivity and its Application to Development and Testing of Electronic Group Support Systems, Tucson.

Briggs, R.O. (2006) The value frequency model: Toward a theoretical understanding of organizational change; in Seifert, S., C. Weinhardt (eds): Group Decision and Negotiation. Karlsruhe, Germany, pp 36-39.

Briggs, R.O. and Vreede, G.J., de (2001) ThinkLets, Building Blocks for Concerted Collaboration.

Briggs, R.O., Adkins, M., Mittleman, D., Kruse, J., Miller, S., Nunamaker, J.F. Jr. (1998), A Technology Transition Model Derived from Field Investigation of GSS Use Aboard the U.S.S. CORONADO, *Journal of MIS*, 15 (3), 151-195.

Briggs, R.O., de Vreede, G.J., & Nunamaker, J.F. Jr. (2003). Collaboration Engineering with ThinkLets to Pursue Sustained Success with Group Support Systems. Journal of Management Information Systems, 19, 31-63.

Briggs, R.O., G.J. de Vreede (2001) ThinkLets: Building blocks for concerted collaboration. Tucson, GroupSystems.com.

Briggs, R.O., G.L. Kolfschoten, G.-J. de Vreede, D.L. Dean (2006) Defining key concepts for collaboration engineering: 12th Americas Conference on Information Systems (AMCIS-12). Acapulco, Mexico

Briggs, R.O., Kolfschoten, G.L., & Vreede, G.J. de. 2005. Toward a Theoretical Model of Consensus Building. Paper presented at the Americas Conference on Information Systems, Omaha, Nebraska, USA, August 11-14).

Briggs, R.O., M. Adkins, D. Mittleman, J. Kruse, S. Miller, J.F. Nunamaker Jr. (1998/1999) A technology transition model derived from field investigation of GSS use aboard the U.S.S. CORONADO. Journal of Management Information Systems 15(3): 151-195.

Briggs, R.O., Murphy, J.D., (in press), Discovering and Evaluating Collaboration Engineering Opportunities: An Interview Protocol Based on the Value Frequency Model, Group Decision and Negotiation.

Briggs, R.O., Vreede G.J. de, Nunamaker, J.F. Jr., Tobey, D. (2001), 'ThinkLets: Achieving Predictable, Repeatable Patterns of Group Interaction with GSS', Proceedings of the 34th HICSS, Los Alamitos: IEEE Society Press.

Briggs, R.O., Vreede, G.J. de and Nunamaker, J.F. Jr. (2003) Collaboration Engineering With ThinkLets To Pursue Sustained Success With Group Support Systems, Journal Of Management Information Systems, 19,(4) 31-63.

Briggs, R.O., Vreede, G.J. de, Nunamaker, J.F. Jr. and David, T.H. (2001) ThinkLets: Achieving Predictable, Repeatable Patterns of Group Interaction with Group Support Systems, In Hawaii International Conference on System Sciences IEEE Computer Society Press, Los Alamitos.

Briggs, R.O.; Kolfschoten, G.L.; Vreede, G.J. de and Dean, D.L. (2006). Defining Key Concepts for Collaboration Engineering, Americas Conference on Information Systems, Acapulco, Mexico, AIS.

Briggs, R.O.; Vreede, G.J. de and Nunamaker, J.F. Jr (2003). Collaboration Engineering with ThinkLets to Pursue Sustained Success with Group Support Systems, Journal of Management Information Systems 19,(4): 31-63.

Briggs. R.O., Kolfschoten, G.L., de Vreede, G.J., & Dean, D. L. (2006). Defining key concepts for collaboration engineering. Paper presented at the Americas Conference on Information Systems, Acapulco, Mexico: AIS.

Brown, V. R., & Paulus, P. B. (2002). Making group brainstorming more effective: Recommendations from an associative memory perspective. Current Directions in Psychology Science, 11, 208-212.

Cannon-Bowers, E., and S. A. Converse. 2001. Shared mental models in expert team decision making. Environmental effects on cognitive abilities: 221.

Cataldo, M., P. A Wagstrom, J. D Herbsleb, and K. M Carley. 2006. Identification of coordination requirements: implications for the Design of collaboration and awareness tools. In Proceedings of the 2006 20th anniversary conference on Computer supported cooperative work, 353–362.

Chakrapani, A. (2005), A Design & Evaluation Framework for Setting Up a Community of Practice, Master's Thesis, University of Nebraska at Omaha.

Chambless, P., S. Hasselbauer, S. Loeb, S. Luhrs, D. Newbery, and W. Scherer. 2005. Design recommendation of a collaborative group decision support system for the aerospace corporation. In Systems and Information Engineering Design Symposium, 2005 IEEE, 183-191.

Cheng, K.E., & Deek, F.P. (2007). A Framework for Studying Voting in Group Support Systems, Paper presented at the Hawaii International Conference on System Sciences, Waikoloa: IEEE Computer Society Press.

Christensen, E. (1983). Study Circles: Learning in Small Groups. Journal for Specialists in Group Work, November, 211-217.

Clawson, V.K., Bostrom, R., & Anson, R. (1993). The Role of the Facilitator in Computer-Supported Meetings. Small Group Research, 24(4), 547-565.

Clawson, V.K., Bostrom, R.P. (1996), ' Research Driven Facilitation Training for Computer Supported Environments'. Group Decision and Negotiation, No. 1, 7–29.

Cohen, S. G. and Bailey, D. E. 1997. "What Makes Teams Work: Group Effectiveness Research from the Shop Floor to the Executive Suite," Journal of Management (23:3), June 1, pp. 239-290.

Connolly, T., Jessup, L.M., & Valacich, J.S. 1990. "Effects of Anonymity and Evaluative Tone on Idea Generation in Computer-Mediated Groups." Management Science, 36(6), 689-703.

Corbitt, G., L. Wright, M. Christopolous (2000) New approaches to business process redesign: A case study of collaborative group technology and service mapping. Group Decision and Negotiation 9(2): 97-107.

Creswell, J.W. (1998), Qualitative Inquiry and Research Design: Choosing Among Five Traditions, Thousand Oaks, CA: Sage.

Culnan, M.J., Markus, M.L. (1987) 'Information Technologies'. In F.M. Jablin, L.L. Putnam, K.H. Roberts, L.W. Porter (eds)., Handbook of Organizational Communication - An Interdisciplinary Perspective (pp. 420-443), Sage Publications, London, United Kingdom.

Datta, D. 2007. Sustainability of community-based organizations of the rural poor: Learning from Concern's rural development projects, Bangladesh. Community Development Journal 42, no. 1: 47.

Davis, A., Murphy, J., Owens, D., Khazanchi, D. and Zigurs, I. 2009. "Avatars, People, and Virtual Worlds: Foundations for Research in Metaverses," Journal of the Association for Information Systems (10:2), pp. 90-117.

Davison, R.M., Briggs, R.O. (2000), GSS for Presentation Support, Communications of the ACM, 43, 9, 91-97.

de Vreede. G.J. (1995) Facilitating Organizational Change - The Participative Application of Dynamic Modelling, Doctoral Dissertation, Delft University of Technology, The Netherlands.

de Vreede, G.J. (2001), A Field Study into the Organizational Application of GSS, Journal of Information Technology Cases & Applications, 2(4).

de Vreede, G.J. (2010), ISQA-8250 Facilitation of Collaborative Problem Solving, Handouts, University of Nebraska at Omaha.

de Vreede, G.J., Boonstra, J., & Niederman, F. (2002). What is effective GSS facilitation: A qualitative inquiry into participants' perceptions, Proceedings of the 38th Hawaiian International Conference on System Sciences, Los Alamitos: IEEE Computer Society Press.

de Vreede, G.J., R.O. Briggs (1997) Meetings of the Future: Enhancing Group Collaboration with Group Support Systems.

de Vreede, G.J. & Briggs, R.O. (2005). Collaboration Engineering: Designing repeatable processes for high-value collaborative tasks, Hawaii International Conference on System Science, Los Alamitos: IEEE Computer Society Press.

de Vreede, G.J., Briggs, R.O. (2005), Collaboration Engineering: Designing Repeatable Processes for High-Value Collaborative Tasks, Proceedings of the 38th Hawaiian International Conference on System Sciences, Los Alamitos: IEEE Computer Society Press.

de Vreede, G.J., Briggs, R.O., Duin, van, R., Enserink, B. (2000), 'Athletics in Electronic Brainstorming: Asynchronous Electronic Brainstorming in Very Large Groups', Proceedings 33rd HICSS, Los Alamitos: IEEE Computer Society Press.

de Vreede, G.J., Briggs, R.O., Massey, A. (2009), Collaboration Engineering: Foundations and Opportunities, Journal of the Association of Information Systems, (10:3), 121-137.

de Vreede, G.J. and Bruijn, J.A. de (1999) Exploring the boundaries of successful GSS Application: Supporting inter-organizational policy networks., DataBase, 30,(3-4) 111-131.

de Vreede, G.J., Davison, R., Briggs, R.O. (2001), How A Silver Bullet May Lose Its Shine: Learning from Failures with Group Support Systems, working paper, Delft University of Technology.

de Vreede, G.J., Davison, R. and Briggs, R.O. (2003) How a Silver Bullet May Lose its Shine - Learning from Failures with Group Support Systems, Communications of the ACM, 46,(8) 96-101.

de Vreede, G.J., Jones, N., Mgaya, R. (1998), Exploring the Application and Acceptance of Group Support Systems in Africa, *Journal of Management Information Systems*, 15 (3), 197-234.

de Vreede, G.J., Kolfschoten, G.L., & Briggs, R.O. (2006). ThinkLets: A collaboration engineering pattern language. International Journal of Computerized Applications in Technology, 25, 140-154.

de Vreede, G.J., P.C. Muller (1997), Why Some GSS Meetings Just Don't Work: Exploring Success Factors of Electronic Meetings, Proceedings of the 7th ECIS, Cork, Ireland, Vol. III, 1266-1285.

de Vreede, G. J., Niederman, F. and Paarlberg, I. (2002) Towards an instrument to measure participants' perceptions on facilitation in group support systems meetings, Group Decision and Negotiation, 11, 127-144.

de Vreede, G.J., Sol, H.G. (1994) 'Combating Organized Crime with Groupware - Facilitating User Involvement in Information System Development.' In D. Coleman, P.R. Huckle (eds) Proceedings of the GroupWare'94 Europe Conference (pp. 105-118), The Conference Group, Hants, United Kingdom.

de Vreede, G.J., Vogel, D., Kolfschoten, G., & Wien, J. (2003). Fifteen years of GSS in the field: A comparison across time and national boundaries. Proceedings of the Hawaiian Conference on System Sciences, IEEE Computer Science Press.

de Vreede, G.J.; and Wijk, W.B. van, "A Field Study into the Organizational Application of Group Support Systems", *Proceedings of the ACM SIGCPR 1997 Conference*, San Francisco, April 1997.

Dean, D. L., Hender, J. M. Rodgers, T. L. and Santanen, E. 2006. "Identifying Quality, Novel, and Creative Ideas: Constructs and Scales for Idea Evaluation," Journal of Association for Information Systems (7:1), pp. 649-699.

Dean, D. L., Orwig, R.E., & Vogel, D.R. 2000. "Facilitation Methods for Collaborative Modeling Tools." Group Decision and Negotiation, 9(2), 109-127.

Dean, D., Lee, J., Orwig, R., Vogel, D. (1994) 'Technological Support for Group Process Modeling', Journal of Management Information Systems, Vol. 11, pp. 43-63.

Dean, D.L., A. Deokar, R. ter Bush (2006) Making the collaboration engineering investment decision: 39th Hawaii International Conference on System Sciences.

Dean, D.L., J.D. Lee, R.E. Orwig, D.R. Vogel (1994/1995) Technological support for group process modeling. Journal of Management Information Systems 11(3): 43-63.

Dean, D.L., R. Orwig, D.R. Vogel (2000) Facilitation Methods for Collaborative Modeling Tools. Group Decision and Negotiation 9(2): 109-127.

Dean, J.W. Jr. and Sharfman, M.P. (1996). Does Decision Process Matter? A Study of Strategic Decision-Making Effectiveness. The Academy of Management Journal, April. 39 (2), pp. 368-396.

Dennis, A.R. (1994) 'Electronic Support for Large Groups', Journal of Organizational Computing, Vol. 4, pp. 177-197.

Dennis, A.R., & Wixom, B.H. (2002). Investigating the Moderators of the Group Support Systems Use with Meta-Analysis. Journal of Management Information Systems, 18(3), 235-257.

Dennis, A.R., (1994). Electronic support for large groups. Journal of Organizational Computing, 4(2), 177-197.

Dennis, A.R., G.S. Hayes, R.M.J. Daniels (1999) Business process modeling with group support systems. Journal of Management Information Systems 15(4): 115-142.

Dennis, A.R., Haley, B.J., & Vandenberg, R.J., (1996). A meta-analysis of effectiveness, efficiency, and participant satisfaction in GSS research. Proceedings of ICIS 1996, Cleveland, 278-289.

Dennis, A.R., Heminger, A., Nunamaker, J. & Vogel, D., (1990). Bringing automated support to large groups: The Burr-Brown experience. Information and Management, 18(3),111-121.

Dennis, A.R., Nunamaker, J.F. Jr., Vogel, D.R. (1991) 'A Comparison of Laboratory and Field Research in the Study of Electronic Meetings Systems', Journal of Management Information Systems, Vol. 7, pp. 107-135.

Dennis, A.R., Valacich, J.S., Carte, T.A., Garfield, M.M., Haley, B.J., & Aronson, J.E. (1997). The effectiveness of multiple dialogs in electronic brainstorming. Information Systems Research, 8, 203–211.

Dennis, A.R.; George, J.; Jessup, L.; Nunamaker, J.; Vogel, D., "Information Technology to Support Electronic Meetings", MIS Quarterly, 12(4), 1988, 591-624.

Dennis, A.R.; Nunamaker, J.; Vogel, D., A Comparison of Laboratory and Field Research in the Study of Electronic Meeting Systems, Journal of MIS, 7(3), 1991, 107-135.

Dennis, A.R.; Wixom, B.H. and Vandenberg, R.J. (2001). Understanding Fit and Appropriation Effects in Group Support Systems Via Meta-Analysis, Management Information Systems Quarterly 25, (2): 167-183.

DeSanctis, G., and R. B Gallupe. (1987). A foundation for the study of group decision support systems. Management science (33:5), pp 589–609.

DeSanctis, G., M.S. Poole (1994) Capturing the complexity in advanced technology use: Adaptive structuration theory. Organization Science *5(2)*: 121-147.

DeSanctis, G., Poole, M. S., Lewis, H., Desharnais, G. (1992). Using computing in quality team meetings: Some initial observations from the IRS-Minnesota project. *Journal of MIS*, 8(3), 7-26.

Dewey, J. (1910). How we think. Oxford England: Heath.

Dickson, G., Limayem, M., Lee Partridge J., DeSanctis, G. (1996), 'Facilitating Computer Supported Meetings: A Cumulative Analysis In A Multiple Criteria Task Environment'. Group Decision and Negotiation, 5(1), 51-72.

Dickson, G.W., Lee-Partridge, J.E., Robinson, L.H. (1993) 'Exploring Modes of Facilitative Support for GDSS Technology', MIS Quarterly, Vol. 17, pp. 173-194.

Dickson, G.W., Partridge, J.L., and Robinson, L.H. (1993). 'Exploring Modes of Facilitative Support for GDSS Technology'. MIS Quarterly, June, p.173-194.

Diehl, M., & Stroebe, W. (1987). Productivity loss in idea-generating groups: Tracking down the blocking effect. Journal of Personality and Social Psychology, 61, 392-403.

Drach-Zahavy, A. & Stomech, A. (2001). Understanding team innovation: The role of team processes and structures. Group Dynamics: Theory, Research, and Practice, 5, 111-123.

Drucker, P.F. (1989) The New Realities, Harper and Row, New York.

D'zurilla, T.J. and Goldfried, M.R. (1971). Problem Solving and Behavior Modification. Journal of Abnormal Psychology. 78 (1), pp. 107-126.

References

Easton, G.K., George, J.F., Nunamaker, J.F., Jr., & Pendergast, M.O. (1990). Using two different electronic meeting system tools for the same task: An experimental comparison. Journal of Management Information Systems, 7, 85–99.

Ebersbach, A., Glaser, M. and Heigl, R. 2008. Wiki: Web Collaboration, New York, Springer-Verlag Inc.

Eden, C. (1990). 'The Unfolding Nature of Group Decision Support. In C. Eden, J. Radford (Eds.), Tackling Strategic Problems-The Role of Group Decision Support. Sage.

Eden, C. (1995) "On evaluating the performance of 'wide-band' GDSS's," *European Journal of Operational Research*, 81, 302-311.

Emery, C.C. Jr. Ree(1994). Engineering the requirements process for executive Support System development using an electronic meeting system", Proceedings of HICSS 1994, 4, 41-50, IEEE Computer Society Press, Los Alamitos CA.

Emery, C.C. Jr., "Reengineering the Requirements Process for Executive Support System Development Using an Electronic Meeting System", *Proceedings of HICSS 1994*, Volume IV, 1994, pp. 41-50, IEEE Computer Society Press, Los Alamitos CA.

Evans, C. R. and Dion, K. L. 1991. "Group Cohesion and Performance: A Meta-analysis," Small Group Research (22:2), p. 175.

Evans, P., B. Wolf (2005) Collaboration rules. Harvard Business Review *83(7/8)*: 96-104.

Fjermestad, J. and Hiltz, S.R. (1999) An Assessment of Group Support Systems Experimental Research: Methodology and Results, Journal Of Management Information Systems, 15,(3) 7-149.

Fjermestad, J. and Hiltz, S.R. (2001). A Descriptive Evaluation of Group Support Systems Case and Field Studies, Journal of Management Information Systems 17, (3): 115-159.

Fjermestad, J. and Hiltz, S.R. 2000. "Group Support Systems: A Descriptive Evaluation of Case and Field Studies. Journal of Management Information Systems, 2001 (17:3), pp. 115-159.

Fjermestad, J., & Hiltz, S.R. (1998),.An assessment of Group Support Systems experimental research: Methodology and results. Journal of Management Information Systems, 15 (3), 7-149.

Fjermestad, J., Hiltz, S.R. (2000), A Descriptive Evaluation of Group Support Systems Case and Field Studies, Journal of Management Information Systems,17(3).

Flores, F., M. Graves, B. Hartfield, and T. Winograd, Computer Systems and the Design of Organizational Interaction, ACM Transactions on Office Information Systems, Vol. 6, No. 2, pp. 153-172, 1988.

Fruhling, A., Vreede, G.J. de (2005), Collaborative Usability Testing to Facilitate Stakeholder Involvement, in: S. Biffl, A. Aurum, B. Boehm, H. Erdogmus, P. Grünbacher (eds), Value Based Software Engineering, Berlin: Springer-Verlag, 201-223.

Fulk, J. and DeSanctis, G. (1995) Electronic Communication for Changing Organizational Forms, Organization Science, 6,(4) 337-349.

Gallupe, B.; DeSanctis, G. and Dickson, G. "Computer-based Support for Group Problem Finding: An Experimental Investigation," MIS Quarterly, 12(2), 1988, 277-296.

Gallupe, R.B., Dennis, A.R, Cooper, W.H., Valacich, J.S. , Nunamaker, J.F. and Bastianutti, L. (1992) Group Size and Electronic Brainstorming, Academy of Management Journal, 35350-369.

Gamma, E., Helm, R., Johnson, R. and Vlissides, J. (1995) Elements of Reusable Object-Oriented Software, Addison-Wesley Publishing Company.

Gavish, B., & Gerdes, J.H. 1997. "Voting Mechanisms and Their Implications in a GDSS Environment." Annals of Operation Research, 71(1), 41-74.

George, J.F., Nunamaker, J.F. Jr., & Valacich, J.S., (1992). Electronic meeting systems as innovation. Information & Management, 22(3), 187-195.

Golder, S. A, and B. A Huberman. 2006. Usage patterns of collaborative tagging systems. Journal of Information Science 32, no. 2: 198.

Graaff, J. de, Appelman, J.H., Verburg, R.M., Jordan, R. (2005), Group supported knowledge elicitation: where Knowledge Management meets Groups Support Systems, Proceedings of Group Decision & Negotiation 2005, Vienna, Austria, July 10-13.

Gray, P., Vogel, D., & Beauclair, R., (1990). Assessing GDSS empirical research. European Journal of Operations Research, Spring 1990.

Griffith, T., Fuller M., Northcraft G. (1998), 'Facilitator Influence in Group Support Systems'. Information Systems Research, 9(1), 20-36.

Grisé, M., & Gallupe, R. B. 2000. "Information Overload: Addressing the Productivity Paradox in Face-to-Face Electronic Meetings." Journal of Management Information Systems, 16(3), 157-185.

Grisé, Mary-Liz, and R. Brent Gallupe. 1999. Information overload: addressing the productivity paradox in face-to-face electronic meetings. J. Manage. Inf. Syst. 16, no. 3: 157-185.

Grohowski, R. , McGoff, C. , Vogel, D., Martz, B. and Nunamaker, J. (1990) Implementing Electronic Meeting Systems at IBM: Lessons Learned and Success Factors, Management Information Systems Quarterly, 14,(4) 368–383.

Grünbacher, P., Köszegi, S., Biffl, S. (2005), Stakeholder Value Proposition Elicitation and Reconciliation, in: S. Biffl, A. Aurum, B. Boehm, H. Erdogmus, P. Grünbacher (eds), Value Based Software Engineering, Berlin: Springer-Verlag, 133-154.

Guilford, J. (1967). Creativity: Yesterday, today, and tomorrow. Journal of Creative Behavior, 1, 3-14.

Hahn, J., J. Y Moon, and C. Zhang. 2008. Emergence of New Project Teams from Open Source Software Developer Networks: Impact of Prior Collaboration Ties◊. Information Systems Research 19, no. 3: 369.

Harder, R.J., Higley, H. (2004), Application of ThinkLets to Team Cognitive Task Analysis, Proceedings of the 37th Hawaii International Conference On System Sciences, IEEE Computer Society Press.

Harder, R.J., Keeter, J.M., Woodcock, B.W., Ferguson, J.W., Wills, F.W. (2005), Insights in Implementing Collaboration Engineering, Proceedings of the 38th Hawaiian International Conference on System Sciences, Los Alamitos: IEEE Computer Society Press.

Harrison, B.N. and Coplien, J.O. (1996) Patterns of Productive Software Organizations, Bell Labs Technical Journal.

Hayne, S.C. (1999). The Facilitator's Perspective on Meetings and Implications for Group Support Systems Design. Database, 30(3-4), 72-91.

Herik, C.W. van den, & de Vreede, G.J. (1997). GSS for cooperative policymaking: No trivial matter. Proceedings of the ACM Group 1997 Conference, Phoenix, Arizona. November 1997.

Higgs, M., U. Plewnia, and J. Ploch. 2005. Influence of team composition and task complexity on team performance. Team Performance Management 11, no. 7/8: 227.

Hoegl, M., Weinkauf, K., & Gemuenden, H. (2004). Interteam Coordination, Project Commitment, and Teamwork in Multiteam R&D Projects: A Longitudinal Study. Organization Science, 15(1), 38-55. doi:10.1287/orsc.1030.0053.

Hofstede, G. (1980) Culture's consequences: International differences in work-related values, Sage, Beverly Hills, USA.

Hollingshead, A.B., McGrath, J.E., & O'Connor, K.M. (1993). Group task performance and communication technology: A longitudinal study of computer-mediated versus face-to-face groups. Small Group Research, 24,3307–333.

Huber, G.P. and McDaniel, R (1986) The Decision Making Paradigm of Organizational Design, Management Science, 32,(5) 572-589.

Hwang, M.I. (1998). Did Task Type Matter in the Use of Decision Room GSS? A Critical Review and a Meta-analysis. International Journal of Management Science, 26(1), 1-15.

Janis, I. L. (1972). Victims of groupthink. Boston: Houghton Mifflin.

Jarvenpaa, S.L., Rao,, V.S., & Huber, G.P. (1988). Computer support for meetings of medium-sized groups working on unstructured problems: A field experiment, MIS Quarterly, 12, 645-666.

Jessup, L.M., Valacich, J.S. (eds.) (1993). Group Support Systems: New Perspectives, New York: Macmillan.

Jones, A.N.; and Miller, L., "Using Technology for Stakeholder Consultation - The World Bank's Use of GroupSystems V in Developing Countries", Proceedings of HCISS 1997, 1997, 464-468.

References

Kamrani, A. K, and E. S Abouel Nasr. 2008. Product design and development framework in collaborative engineering environment. International Journal of Computer Applications in Technology 32, no. 2: 85–94.

Kellermanns, Franz W., Steven W. Floyd, Allison W. Pearson, and Barbara Spencer. 2008. The contingent effect of constructive confrontation on the relationship between shared mental models and decision quality. Journal of Organizational Behavior 29, no. 1: 119-137. doi:10.1002/job.497.

Khazanchi, D. and Zigurs, I. (2006). Patterns for effective management of virtual projects: Theory and evidence, International Journal of e-Collaboration 2,(3): 25-48.

Kolfschoten, G.L. & de Vreede, G.J. (2007). ThinkLet based Collaboration Process Design.

Kolfschoten, G.L. and Veen, W. (2005) Tool Support for GSS Session Design, In Hawaii International Conference on System Sciences IEEE Computer Society Press, Los Alamitos.

Kolfschoten, G.L., & Vreede, G.J. de (2009). A Design Approach for Collaboration Processes: A Multi-Method Design Science Study in Collaboration Engineering. Journal of Management Information Systems, 26(1), 225-257.

Kolfschoten, G.L., Appelman, J.H., Briggs, R.O. and Vreede, G.J. de (2004a) Recurring Patterns of Facilitation Interventions in GSS Sessions, In Hawaii International Conference On System Sciences IEEE Computer Society Press, Los Alamitos.

Kolfschoten, G.L., Briggs, R.O., Appelman, J.H. and Vreede, G.J. de (2004b) ThinkLets as Building Blocks for Collaboration Processes: A Further Conceptualization, In CRIWG, Vol. LNCS 3198 (Eds, Vreede, G.J. de, Guerrero, L.A. and Raventos, G.M.) Springer-Verlag, San Carlos, Costa Rica, pp. 137-152.

Kolfschoten, G.L., G.-J. de Vreede, A. Chakrapani, P. Koneri (2006b) The collaboration engineering approach for designing collaboration processes; in Briggs, R.O., J.F. Nunamaker Jr. (eds): First HICSS Symposium on Case and Field Studies of Collaboration. Poipu, Kauai, Hawaii.

Kolfschoten, G.L., R.O. Briggs, G.J.de Vreede, P.H.M. Jacobs, J.H. Appelman (2006a) A Conceptual Foundation of the thinkLet Concept for Collaboration Engineering. International Journal of Human-Computer Studies 64: 11.

Kolfschoten, G.L., Vreede, G.J. de, (in press), A Design Approach for Collaboration Engineering: A Multi-Method Design Science Study in Collaboration Engineering, Journal of Management Information Systems.

Kolfschoten, G.L.; Vreede, G.J. de and Pietron, L. (in press). A training approach for the transition of repeatable collaboration processes to practitioners, Group Decision and Negotiation.

Kollar, I., F. Fischer, and F. Hesse. 2006. Collaboration Scripts – A Conceptual Analysis. Educational Psychology Review 18, no. 2 (June 1): 159-185.

Kollar, I., F. Fischer, and J. D Slotta. 2005. Internal and external collaboration scripts in web-based science learning at schools. In Proceedings of the 2005 conference on Computer support for collaborative learning: learning 2005: the next 10 years!, 331–340.

Kozlowski, S., & Bell, B. (2008). Team learning, development, and adaptation. Work group learning: Understanding, improving and assessing how groups learn in organizations (pp. 15-44). New York, NY: Taylor & Francis Group/Lawrence Erlbaum Associates.

Krcmar, H., Lewe, H., & Schwabe, G., (1994). Empirical CATeam research in meetings. Proceedings of HICSS 1994, 31-40, IEEE Computer Society Press, Los Alamitos, CA.

Krcmar, H.; Lewe, H.; and Schwabe, G., "Empirical CATeam Research in Meetings", *Proceedings of HICSS 1994*, 1994, 31-40, IEEE Computer Society Press, Los Alamitos CA.

Larey, T. S., & Paulus, P. B. (1999). Group preference and convergent tendencies in small groups: A content analysis of group brainstorming performance. Creativity Research Journal, 12, 175-184.

Laukkanen, Sanna, Annika Kangas, and Jyrki Kangas. 2002. Applying voting theory in natural resource management: a case of multiple-criteria group decision support. Journal of Environmental Management 64, no. 2 (February): 127-137. doi:10.1006/jema.2001.0511.

Laxmisan, A., F. Hakimzada, O. R Sayan, R. A Green, J. Zhang, and V. L Patel. 2007. The multitasking clinician: decision-making and cognitive demand during and after team handoffs in emergency care. International journal of medical informatics (76: 11-12), pp. 801–811.

Levi, D. 2007. Group dynamics for teams. Sage Publications, Inc.

References

Limayem, M., Lee-Patridge, J.E., Dickson, G.W., DeSanctis, G.D. (1993) 'Enhancing GDSS Effectiveness: Automated versus Human Facilitation.' In J.F. Nunamaker Jr. R.H. Sprague (eds) Proceedings of the 26th Hawaiian International Conference on System Sciences (Volume IV, pp. 95-101), IEEE Computer Society Press, Los Alamitos CA, USA.

Litchfield, R. C. (2008). Brainstorming reconsidered: A goal-based view. Academy of Management Review, 33, 649-688.

Lodewijkx, Hein F. M., Jacob M. Rabbie, and Lieuwe Visser. 2006. "Better to be safe than to be sorry": Extinguishing the individual – group discontinuity effect in competition by cautious reciprocation. European Review of Social Psychology 17: 185.

Lukosch, S. and Schümmer, T. (2004) Communicating design knowledge with groupware technology patterns, In CRIWG 2004, Vol. LNCS 3198 (Ed, Vreede, G.J. de, Guerrero, L.A., Raventos, G.M., (eds.) Springer-Verlag, San Carlos, Costa Rica, pp. 223-237.

Martz, B.; Vogel, D. and Nunamaker, J., "Electronic Meeting Systems: Results from the Field," *Decision Support Systems*, April 1992.

McLeod, P.L. (1992). An Assessment of the Experimental Literature on Electronic Support of Group Work: Results of a Meta-Analysis. Human-Computer Interaction, 7, 257-280.

Mejias, R.; Shepherd, M.; Vogel, D.; and Lazaneo, L. "Consensus and Perceived Satisfaction Levels: A Cross-Cultural Comparison of GSS and non-GSS Outcomes Within and Between the U.S. and Mexico," *Journal of MIS*, 13(3), 1997, pp. 137-161.

Miranda, S.M., Bostrom, R.P. (1999), 'Meeting Facilitation: Process Versus Content Interventions'. Journal of Management Information Systems, 15(4), 89-114.

Mitroff, I.I., Betz, F., Pondly, L.R., and Sagasty, F. On Managing Science In The Systems Age: Two Schemas For The Study Of Science As A Whole Systems Phenomenon. TIMS Interfaces, 4, 3 (1974), 46-58.

Mittleman, D. D, R. O Briggs, J. Murphy, and A. Davis. 2009. Toward a Taxonomy of Groupware Technologies. Lecture Notes In Computer Science: 305–317.

Montoya-Weiss, M. M, A. P Massey, and M. Song. 2001. Getting it together: Temporal coordination and conflict management in global virtual teams. Academy of Management Journal: 1251–1262.

Mulder, I., Swaak, J., & Kessels, J. 2002. "Assessing learning and shared understanding in technology-mediated interaction." Educational Technology & Society, 5(1), 35-47.

Mumford, M. D., Reiter-Palmon, R., & Redmond, M. R. (1994). Problem construction and cognition: Applying problem representations in ill-defined domains. In M.A. Runco (Ed.), Problem finding, problem solving, and creativity (pp. 3-39). Norwood, NJ: Ablex.

Mumford, M., Mobley, M., Uhlman, C., & Reiter-Palmon, R. (1991). Process analytic models of creative capacities. Creativity Research Journal, 4, 91-122.

Munkvold, B.E., I. Zigurs (2005) Integration of e-collaboration technologies: Research opportunities and challenges. International Journal of e-Collaboration 1(2): 1-24.

Newell, A., & Simon, H. (1972). Human problem solving. Englewood Cliffs, New Jersey: Prentice-Hall.

Nguyen, D. T. and Canny, J., 2007. "Multiview: Improving Trust in Group Video Conferencing Through Spatial Faithfulness," in Proceedings of the SIGCHI Conference on Human Factors in Computing Systems, ACM, San Jose, CA, pp. 1465-1474. Available at: http://portal.acm.org/citation.cfm?id=1240624.1240846 [Accessed May 5, 2009].

Niederman, F., Beise , C.M., Beranek, P.M. (1996), 'Issues and Concerns about Computer-Supported Meetings: The Facilitator's Perspective'. MISQ, 20(1), 1-22.

Niegemann, H.M. and Domagk, S. (2005) ELEN Project Evaluation Report, University of Erfurt, Erfurt, http://www2tisip.no/E-LEN.

Nunamaker, J.F. Jr., Applegate, L.M., & Konsynski, B.R. (1987). Facilitating group creativity: Experience with a Group Decision Support System. Journal of MIS, 3(4), 5-19.

Nunamaker, J.F. Jr., Briggs, R.O., Mittleman, D.D., Vogel, D. and Balthazard, P.A. (1997) Lessons from a Dozen Years of Group Support Systems Research: A Discussion of Lab and Field Findings, Journal of Management Information Systems, 13,(3) 163-207.

Nunamaker, J.F. Jr., Briggs, R.O., Mittleman, D.D., Vogel, D.D., Balthazard, P.A. (1996). Lessons from a Dozen Years of Group Support Systems Research: A Discussion of Lab and Field Findings. Journal of Management Information Systems, Winter 1996-1997. 13 (3), pp 163-207.

Nunamaker, J.F. Jr., Dennis, A., Valacich, J., Vogel, D., George, J.F. (1991). Electronic Meeting Systems to Support Group Work, Communications of the ACM, 34(7), 40-61.

Nunamaker, J.F. Jr., Vogel, D.R., Heminger, A., Martz, B., Grohowski, R., & McGoff, C. (1989) .Experiences at IBM with Group Support Systems: A field study. Decision Support Systems, 5(2) ,183-196.

Nunamaker, J.F., Briggs, R.O., Mittleman, D. (1995) 'Ten Years of Lessons Learned with Group Support Systems.' In D. Coleman, R. Khanna (eds) Groupware: Technologies and Applications (pp. 146-193), Prentice Hall, Saddle River, NJ, USA.

Nunamaker, J.F., R.O. Briggs, G.-J. de Vreede (2001) From information technology to value creation technology; in Dickson, G.W., G. DeSanctis (eds): Information technology and the new enterprise: New models for managers, Prentice Hall.

Nunamaker, Jr., J., Briggs, R., Mittleman, D., Vogel, D., & Balthazard, P. (1997). Lessons from a dozen years of group support systems research: a discussion of lab and field finding, Journal of Management Information Systems, Vol. 13, No. 3, pp. 163-207.

Osborn, A. F. 1963. Applied Imagination, 3rd ed. New York, NY: Charles Scribner's Sons.

Paas, F., Renkl, A., & Sweller, J. (2003). Cognitive load theory and instructional design: Recent developments. Educational Psychologist, 38(1), 1-4. doi:10.1207/S15326985EP3801_1.

Penichet, V. M. R., I. Marin, J. A. Gallud, M. D. Lozano, and R. Tesoriero. 2007. A classification method for CSCW systems. Electronic Notes in Theoretical Computer Science 168: 237–247.

Pervan, G., and D. Arnott. 2006. Key Issues for GSS Research. In Group Decision and Negotiation (GDN) 2006 International Conference, Karlsruhe, Germany, June 25-28, 2006; Proceedings, 78.

Pervan, G.P. (1998) A review of research in Group Support Systems: Leaders, approaches and directions. Decision Support Systems,.149-159.

Pinsonneault, A., Barki, H., Gallupe, B. and Hoppen, N. (1999) Electronic Brainstorming: the Illusion of Productivity, Information Systems Research, 10,(2) 110-133.

Pinsonneault, A., K.L. Kraemer (1989) The impact of technological support on groups: an assessment of the empirical research. Decision Support Systems 5: 197-216.

Poltrock, S., J. Grudin (1994) Computer supported cooperative work and groupware: Conference on Human Factors in Computing Systems. Boston, MA.

Poole, S., DeSanctis, G., Kirsch, L., & Jackson, M. (1991). An observational study of everyday use of a Group Decision Support System, Proceedings of HICSS 1991. IEEE Computer Society Press, Los Alamitos, CA.

Poole, S.; DeSanctis, G.; Kirsch, L., Jackson, M. An Observational Study of Everyday Use of a Group Decision Support System, *Proceedings of HICSS 1991*. IEEE Computer Society Press, Los Alamitos CA

Post, B.Q. (1993). A business case framework for group support technology. Journal of Management Information Systems, 9(3), 1993, 7-26.

Post, B.Q. (1992) 'Building the Business Case for Group Support Technology.' In J.F. Nunamaker Jr. R.H. Sprague (eds) Proceedings of the 25th Hawaiian International Conference on System Sciences (Volume IV, pp. 34-45), IEEE Computer Society Press, Los Alamitos CA, USA.

Ravi Beegun, R. B, and P. Leroy. 2009. Risk management challenges in UCITS III funds. Journal of Securities Operations & Custody 2, no. 1: 37–52.

Reinig, B. A, R. O Briggs, and J. F Nunamaker. 2007. On the measurement of ideation quality. Journal of Management Information Systems 23, no. 4: 143–161.

Reiter-Palmon, R., M. D Mumford, J. O.C Boes, and M. A Runco. 1997. Problem construction and creativity: The role of ability, cue consistency, and active processing. Creativity Research Journal 10, no. 1: 9–23.

References

Ren, Yuqing, Sara Kiesler, and Susan R. Fussell. 2008. "Multiple Group Coordination in Complex and Dynamic Task Environments: Interruptions, Coping Mechanisms, and Technology Recommendations." Journal of Management Information Systems (25: 1), pp. 105-130.

Riemen, D.J. (1986), The essential structure of caring interaction: Doing phenomenology, in: Munhall, P.M., Oiler, C.J. (eds), Nursing research: A qualitative perspective, Norwalk, CT: Appleton-Century-Crofts, 85-105.

Rietzschel, E. F, B. A Nijstad, and W. Stroebe. 2006. Productivity is not enough: A comparison of interactive and nominal brainstorming groups on idea generation and selection. Journal of Experimental Social Psychology 42, no. 2: 244–251.

Rising, L. (2001) Design Patterns in Communication Software, Cambridge University Press, Cambridge.

Romano, N.C. Jr., Nunamaker, J.F. Jr., Briggs, R.O., Vogel, D.R. (1997) 'Architecture, Design, and Development of an HTML/Javascript Web-Based Group Support System.' Submitted to the Special Issue of JASIS on Artificial Intelligence Techniques for Emerging Information Systems Applications, 1997.

Runco, M. A, J. J Illies, and R. Reiter-Palmon. 2005. Explicit Instructions to Be Creative and Original-A Comparison of Strategies and Criteria as Targets with Three Types of Divergent Thinking Tests. The Korean Journal of Thinking & Problem Solving 15, no. 1: 5–15.

Saaty, T. L, and J. S Shang. 2007. Group decision-making: Head-count versus intensity of preference. Socio-Economic Planning Sciences 41, no. 1: 22–37.

Sahni, D., J. Van den Bergh, and K. Coninx. 2008. Towards a Collaboration Framework for Selection of ICT Tools.

Saltz, J. S., S. R. Hiltz, M. Turnoff, and K. Passerine. 2007. Increasing participation in distance learning courses. IEEE Internet Computing 11, no. 3: 36–44.

Santanen, E. L, R. O Briggs, and G. J de Vreede. 2000. The cognitive network model of creativity: a new causal model of creativity and a new brainstorming technique. In Proceedings of the 33rd Hawaii International Conference on System Sciences, 7:7004. Vol. 7.

Santanen, E.L. (2005) Resolving Ideation Paradoxes: Seeing Apples as Oranges Through the Clarity of ThinkLets, In Hawaii International Conference on System Sciences IEEE Computer Society Press, Los Alamitos.

Santanen, E.L. and Vreede, G.J. de (2004) Creative Approaches to Measuring Creativity: Comparing the Effectiveness of Four Divergence ThinkLets, In Hawaiian International Conference on System Sciences IEEE Computer Society Press, Los Alamitos.

Santanen, E.L., Vreede, G.J. de and Briggs, R.O. (2004) Causal Relationships in Creative Problem Solving: Comparing Facilitation Interventions for Ideation, Journal Of Management Information Systems, 20,(4) 167 -197.

Schummer, T. and Lukosch, S. 2007. Patterns for Computer-mediated Interaction, Chichester, England: John Wiley and Sons.

Schwenk, C.R. (1984). Cognitive Simplification Processes in Strategic Decision-Making. Strategic Management Journal. Apr-Jun, 5 (2), pp. 111-128.

Shepherd, M.M., Briggs, R.O., Reinig, B.A., Yen, J., & Nunamaker, J.F., Jr. (1997). Social comparison to improve electronic brainstorming: Beyond anonymity. Journal of Management Information Systems, 12, 155–170.

Simon, H.A. (1979). Rational Decision Making in Business Organizations. The American Economic Review. September. 69 (4), pp. 493-513.

Simpson, C. W., and L. Prusak. 1995. Troubles with information overload—moving from quantity to quality in information provision. International Journal of Information Management 15, no. 6: 413–425.

Smith, A. D. 2007. Collaborative commerce through web-based information integration technologies. International Journal of Innovation and Learning 4, no. 2: 127–144.

Sternberg, R. (1986). Intelligence, wisdom, and creativity: Three is better than one. Educational Psychologist, 21, 175-190. doi:10.1207/s15326985ep2103_2

References

Strasser, G., & Titus, W. (1985). Pooling of unshared information in group decision making: Biased information sampling during discussion. Journal of Personality and Social Psychology, 48, 1467-1478.

Support Group Work. Communications of the ACM
34(7): 40-61.

Systems. Journal of Creativity and Innovation Management *6(2)*:
106-116.

Tyran, C., Dennis, A., Vogel, D., & Nunamaker, J. (1992). The application of electronic meeting systems to support strategic management. MIS Quarterly, September, 1992.

Valacich, J. S, L. M Jessup, A. R Dennis, and J. F. Nunamaker. 1992. A conceptual framework of anonymity in group support systems. Group Decision and Negotiation 1, no. 3: 219–241.

Valacich, J.S., Dennis, A.R., Connolly, T. (1994) 'Idea Generation in Computer Based Groups: A New Ending to an Old Story.' Organizational Behavior and Human Decision Processes, Vol. 57, pp. 448-467.

Van Knippenberg, D., and M. C Schippers. 2006. Work group diversity.

Veld, J. I. T. 1987. Analyse van Organisatie Problemen. Leiden: Stenfert Kroese.

Vissers, G., & Dankbaar, B. (2002). Creativity in multidisciplinary new product development teams. Creativity in Development Teams, 11, 31-40.

Vogel, D. & Nunamaker, J., (1990). Group Decision Support System Impact: Multi-Methodological Exploration. Information and Management, 15-28.

Vogel, D.; Nunamaker, J.; Martz, B.; Grohowski, R.; and McGoff, C., "Electronic Meeting System Experience at IBM," *Journal of MIS*, 6(3), Winter 1990, pp. 25-43.

Vroom, V. H. 1995. Work and motivation. Jossey-Bass San Francisco.

Watson, R., DeSanctis, G., Poole, M. (1988). 'Using a GDSS to facilitate group consensus: Some intended and unintended consequences'. MIS Quarterly, 12(3), 463-477

Watson, R., M. Alexander, C. Pollard, R. Bostrom (1994), 'Perceptions of Facilitators of a Keypad-Based GSS, Journal of Organizational Computing, 4(2), 103-125.

Watson, Richard T., Teck Hua Ho, and K. S. Raman. 1994. Culture: a fourth dimension of group support systems. Communications of the ACM 37, no. 10: 44-55.

Watson-Manheim, M.B., K.M. Chudoba, K. Crowston (2002) Discontinuities and continuities: a new way to understand virtual work. Information Technology & People *15(3)*: 191-209.

Weick, K. E, K. M Sutcliffe, and D. Obstfeld. 2005. "Organizing and the process of sensemaking." Organization Science (16: 4); pp 409-421.

Westaby, J. D. 2002. "Identifying Specific Factors Underlying Attitudes Toward Change: Using Multiple Methods to Compare Expectancy-Value Theory to Reasons Theory 1," Journal of Applied Social Psychology (32:5), pp. 1083-1104.

Wheelan, S. A. 2009. Group Size, Group Development, and Group Productivity. Small Group Research 40, no. 2: 247.

Whitten, J. L, L. Bentley, and K. Dittman. 2007. Systems Analysis and Design for the Global Enterprise. McGraw-Hill.

Winograd, T., and F. Flores, Understanding Computers and Cognition: A New Foundation for Design, Norwood, N.J., 1986.

Yeung, A. K, D. O Ulrich, S. W Nason, and M. A Von Glinow. 1999. Organizational learning capability. Oxford University Press, USA.

Zeman, E. (2007) Verizon Wireless Subscribers Send 10 Billion SMSs In June, Probably Have Carpal Tunnel: Information Week.

Zigurs, I. Methodological and Measurement Issues in Group Support Systems Research In: Jessup, L.M. and Valacich, J.S. (ed.) Group Support Systems - New Perspectives. New York: Macmillan Publishing Company, 1993.

Zigurs, I., B.D. Buckland (1998) A theory of task/technology fit and group support systems effectiveness. MIS Quarterly *22(3)*: 313-334.

Zigurs, I., D. Khazanchi (forthcoming) From profiles to patterns: A new view of task-technology fit. Information Systems Management *(forthcoming)*.